Advances in
Teacher Education
Volume 4

Editors:

Lilian G. Katz
University of Illinois
Champaign-Urbana

James D. Raths
University of Vermont

Ablex Publishing Corporation
Norwood, New Jersey 07648

ADVANCES IN TEACHER EDUCATION

series editors
LILIAN G. KATZ
JAMES D. RATHS

University of Illinois, Urbana-Champaign

ISBN: 0-89391-564-5
ISSN: 0748-0067

Ablex Publishing Corporation
355 Chestnut Street
Norwood, New Jersey 07648

Contents

Preface

Considerable attention has been given to the importance of reform in teacher education as part of the general movement to improve education in the United States. To add to the discussion of the issues, we are pleased to present eight chapters on a variety of topics concerning teacher education in this fourth volume in the series on advances in teacher education.

In the opening chapter, Lasley and Watras outline their perspective on how the stage might be set for taking necessary steps to reform teacher education. They detail some of the areas of particular difficulty in realizing most of the reforms of teacher education that have been proposed. They also describe the preconditions for significant change to occur.

Patterson offers a description and analysis of the role of the normal schools in training teachers in the Canadian province of Alberta during most of the first half of this century. Patterson's study reveals that in their 40 years of existence, the normal schools trained 22,000 teachers, many of whom were counted among the leaders in the development of their nation's educational establishment. Teacher-educators in the United States will recognize many similarities in the story of Canada's normal schools with their own schools.

The chapter by McAninch, Katz, and Raths addresses some of the problems of teacher-educators in terms of their membership in two subcultures: the scientific culture and the wider university, and the clinical culture of the practitioners. The authors identify five dimensions on which the two cultures differ and show how the norms of each pull teacher-educators in opposite directions. The implications of the cultural conflict for the treatment and location of teacher education on the campus are discussed.

Grimmett explores ways that teacher-educators might synthesize and utilize the rich store of implications to be drawn from research on teaching in preservice education. He advocates a constructivist approach to helping candidates learn to teach and emphasizes the teacher-educator's role as one of encouraging candidates to develop a habit of reflection. Through reflective processes, candidates can reconstruct their understandings of teaching in the direction of greater maturity and complexity.

Ashton suggests that the greatest hope for schools is that new recruits to the teacher ranks arrive equipped with the most sophisticated approaches available to the profession. Ashton raises serious questions about neophyte teachers' abilities to resist the pressures typical of school environments to engage in the older practices, thus missing the opportunity to encourage candidates to become innovative. Ashton presents some ways this pattern might be changed so that new entrants into the ranks of teaching might contribute to changes that will improve the quality of education offered to school.

Copa examines traditional research on the experiences of beginning teachers and then offers an alternative way of understanding this critical point in teachers' careers. Based on a study of a first-year math teacher's efforts to make sense of her predicaments, Copa asserts that although traditional research on neophytes characterized them as paralyzed by their situation, recent research suggests that it is more appropriate to see beginners as builders of implicit theories of teaching and learning.

Boydell contributes a review of research on supervision of student teaching. Although teacher-education candidates, graduates, and teacher educators generally agree that the student teaching experience is the most critical one of all that are included in training, it is a difficult topic to examine empirically. Boydell's description of alternative approaches to supervision and her summary of the pertinent research may help encourage much needed additional work in this important component of the preparation of teachers.

Evans examines complex issues in the provision of field experiences for candidates and presents a framework to be used for planning that addresses many of the problems identified by researchers and practitioners. Although Evans places her framework in the context of teacher education practices in Jamaica, it is likely to be useful in planning field experiences in many other contexts.

We hope that these chapters will contribute to a deeper understanding of the issues faced by teacher educators as they proceed with the complex processes of reform.

Lilian G. Katz
James D. Raths

September, 1988

Chapter 1
Teacher Education at the Crossroads

Thomas J. Lasley

Professor and Chair,
Department of Teacher Education,
University of Dayton

Joseph Watras

Professor
University of Dayton

Teacher education is currently the focus of attention of a wide variety of constituent and special-interest groups. The attention is not new. Debate concerning the efficacy of teacher education programs has been evidenced at institutional and statewide levels for several decades.

Regrettably, however, the debate has led to few substantive changes. The structure, if not the content, of teacher education programs currently is essentially the same as it was prior to World War II. Such lack of progress is a matter of grave concern for those who have an investment in teaching and teacher education, and is particularly disturbing considering the new knowledge about effective teaching that has evolved since the early 1960s when the first handbook of research on teaching (Gage, 1963) was published.

The situation is good and bad. The good is that critics agree to the need for teacher preparation programs. They have criticized the quality of extant programs (see, for example, Cheney, 1987) and argued, as has occurred in Texas and Virginia, for a reduction in the number of courses devoted to pedagogy, but few critics have espoused the view that pedagogical skills need not be taught at all. The bad is that teacher educators have had a distinct tendency to hope that the criticism would pass. All too often, teacher educators' response to criticism has been to do nothing and to hope that the talk would wear itself out. In the past, such a tactic was understandable because most critics moved quickly to new agenda items. But things do not have to happen this way; the inertia resulting from teacher educator intransigence to change can be overcome. Teacher-educators' response in the 1990s could and should be one of seeking genuine improvement. For this to occur, teacher-educators must recognize four preconditions for improvement.

PRECONDITIONS FOR ACTION

Often, setting the stage for reform is harder than demonstrating accomplishment. This is the case in teacher education. At the present time, those responsible for training teachers seem to go in several directions at once, because teacher-educators do not hold a common view of what constitutes improvement. It may be that a group as diverse as a college faculty will never adopt one definition of the best education for all. Nonetheless, if improvement of professional efficacy is to occur, the following preconditions must be met. The preconditions are drawn from the extant reform literature on teacher education (Lasley, 1986a, 1986b); the broader reform literature on teaching and teacher education (Holmes Group, 1986; Carnegie Forum, 1986); and the personal experiences of the authors.

First Precondition: *Adopt An Independent Stance*
Teacher-educators too frequently use other professions to define what teacher education and teaching should entail. The tendency is long-standing. As early as the 1930s (see Callahan, 1962), educators have compared teaching to business practices. More recently, teachers compare their work with that of doctors. The Holmes report, *Tomorrow's Teachers,* is replete with medical analogies and metaphors comparing teacher-educators to clinical faculty and colleges of education to teaching hospitals. Such comparisons, as Jackson (1987) noted, are misdirective and spurious:

> Those who point to the medical profession as a standard for teachers to emulate doubtless think they are doing teachers a good turn by making the comparison. Here is an enviable goal to which teachers might well aspire, they probably reason. What they fail to realize is that the comparison is ultimately degrading to teachers. It is so not only because the goal is so ridiculously out of reach in social and economic terms as to

be almost cruel in the making but also because the analogy fails to consider all that is unique and ennobling about the teacher's work. More than that, either a medical or an engineering paradigm applied to teaching typically goes hand in hand with an emphasis on narrowly defined methods and techniques. What ultimately emerges is a vision of teaching that is almost exclusively technological in its orientation. (p. 388)

Haberman (1986) argued that to "draw lessons for teaching from other professions, we must take into account the conditions under which those other professions are practiced" (p. 720). Comparisons are a temporary palliative; they seldom evoke a more substantial result. They turn people's attention from the important issues and create a set of tacit assumptions that are not efficacious for autonomous, long-term professional development.

For example, a call for improvement that depends on such comparisons to other professions is *Educating a Profession* (Howsam, Corrigan, Denemark, & Nash, 1976). Published over a decade ago, it has become a map of how teaching might evolve in order to become a profession. Unfortunately, because Howsam et al. compared teaching to other professions, they encouraged educational writers to look at specific criteria as essential ingredients to the emergence of teaching as a profession. As a result, the parts of professional activity (e.g., identification of a discrete knowledge base) overshadow broader issues and the relationship of those issues to collective professional responsibility, a responsibility that might entail a change in current state and local policies that have an effect on educators. Examples of policy changes would include the following: to stop recruiting untrained people into classroom service, to stop certificating persons who have no classroom experience, and to stop assigning teachers to teach in areas for which they do not hold certification. A recent NEA (1987) report suggested, for instance, that in excess of 17% of the teachers in the United States, for at least some portion of the school day, are teaching grades or subjects for which they were not academically prepared.

If teachers are to gain respectability and status, it will be because of demonstrated competence, not because of attempts to emulate other highly regarded professionals. Bok (1987) made this point most succinctly with regard to the efforts of teacher educators to enhance their professional status on campus through imitation of arts and science faculty:

Rather than imitate their colleagues in arts and sciences, they should strive to exemplify the highest standards of instruction and to come forth with challenging new ideas about better methods of instruction, better

ways of assessing student progress, better ways of helping those who find
it difficult to learn. It is by serving as an example of good practice and
a catalyst for educational reform that schools of education are most likely
to attract greater respect and attention within the university as a whole.
(p. 80)

For those educators who feel compelled to use the metaphors of
another profession, let them rely on a profession where the linkage
between knowledge and action is not well defined, perhaps theological
education and the ministry. The task that teachers perform is closer
to that of clerics than to that of physicians; teachers do not heal people
nor dispense medicines. They do perform ceremonies that are instructive, just as is a liturgical ceremony, and they do have to make decisions
based on inferences regarding students' intellectual and affective—some
would argue spiritual—needs. Unfortunately, when educators talk of
the science of teaching, they forget the ritualistic and personal nature
of the teaching profession and think instead about the ways in which
the environment calls out of the student certain responses.

Second Precondition: *Create a Sense of Educative Ownership*
The education of teachers tends to relegate students to a passive role.
Many prospective teachers experience alienation from the subject matter
of teaching because they never have to internalize the theories and
ideas they learn. Pedagogical ideals are viewed by preservice teachers
as idiosyncratic to the college classroom, something for here (the campus) not there (the school classroom). The process of translating, adapt-
ing, and assimilating those ideas for use in elementary and secondary
classrooms is viewed as unnecessary, if not dangerous.

The gap between theory and practice, between research and application, is found in almost every profession. The phenomenon has been
particularly observable in teaching because of the myriad theories
proffered for explaining the teaching and learning process. Because there
are so many options, prospective teachers have matriculated through
programs as though walking past a smorgasbord: They taste a little
of everything but seldom savor anything fully, or more likely, they
take so much that they finish the teacher education curriculum feeling
stuffed rather than nourished.

One way of enabling student ownership is to have students defend
their perspectives and their actions. This can be accomplished, in part,
by forcing prospective teachers to critically examine the practical arguments implicit in their actions (see Fenstermacher, 1987). As an
example, a student teacher might assert the following desires or beliefs:

A. I want my students (sixth graders) to be able to exhibit self-discipline during class activities.
B. The best way for students to acquire self-discipline is to have them experience a rigid classroom structure.
C. The best classroom structure for students is one that is based on a set of clear rules and consequences.
D. The best mechanism for implementing rules and consequences is assertive discipline.

The obligation on the part of the teacher educator is to engage the prospective teacher in dialogue about the premises explicitly stated as part of the practical argument: Is there empirical support for the assertion that the best way for students to acquire self-discipline is through a rigid classroom structure? Is assertive discipline the best means of implementing rules? The research reviewed by the prospective teacher is grounded in the needs and assumptions of the student, not in the a priori structure of the teacher education curriculum.

Unfortunately, many teacher education institutions, in an attempt to ensure that preservice teachers understand the research, present the research separately from the students' own professional aims or from the teaching context. As a result, prospective teachers do not see the knowledge base of teacher education as something that could or should alter their practice once they are in the field. For example, in the PROTEACH program at the University of Florida (Ross & Kyle, 1987) students read selected articles, learn to use the organization and management sections of the Florida Performance Measurement System, and practice observing tapes on which appropriate teacher behaviors are evidenced. Such an approach may develop the appearance of professional competence, but because the approach fails to engender ownership, the sophisticated demeanor the prospective teacher appears to demonstrate may be a veneer of unthinking compliance to what people expect rather than a thoughtful development of considered actions. In situations where a mandated system of performance evaluation is evidenced (e.g., Florida and Georgia), such an approach has limited utility in fostering teacher efficacy. Students working through such a curriculum are cast in passive roles and fail to challenge the fundamental assumptions undergirding positivistic measurement systems. They are undoubtedly more technically proficient but may be less professionally capable of making complex judgments based on their clients'—the students'—needs.

The power of the practical argument perspective is that students must be able to articulate their own beliefs and to test those beliefs about teaching. They begin to see the socially constructed nature of personal and professional knowledge. Students must retain the ownership of their education, for they are not learning entirely new things but grafting new ideas and theories to their own professional consciousness. Further, they will develop a broader perspective regarding what constitutes a valid basis for action. Buchmann (1984) noted:

> When one considers the contribution of research knowledge to teacher education and teaching, it is important to realize that common sense, personal commitment, and external policies (e.g., legal mandates, curriculum guides) can also be valid bases for action. In general, an over reliance on research knowledge will be inappropriate for it is time-bound, theory-dependent, and selective. (p. 422)

Third Precondition: *Recognize the Complexity of the Teaching Process*

Teaching is indeed complex, and teachers must make many difficult decisions during a typical school day. The preoccupation with the knowledge base and with accountability has encouraged the adoption of simplified pedagogy and educational reductionism. Further, it has led to a focus on ends rather than on means; on achievement rather than growth; and on accomplishment rather than development.

Teaching is emerging in the popular educational literature as a linear process, something that moves through discrete steps. The Rosenshine (1987) explicit teaching procedures or the Hunter (1983) seven instructional steps are used in many institutions as the ends of instructional evaluation. Preservice teachers learn the steps, and then during student teaching or field practicums they are evaluated on those skills. The linear approach is reinforced by the reliance school districts place on such packaged approaches. Hence, even in teacher education programs where instructional variability is encouraged, students go into field placements and work with teachers who possess the "right" method of presenting concepts and information. The "right way" mentality has emerged even though the originators of linear approaches often caution readers about the context-specific appropriateness of their techniques. Rosenshine (1986), for example, when asked to critique a content lesson on the Federalist Papers taught by Secretary Bennett, noted:

> Content learning is involved when teachers learn how the planets were formed, the causes of volcanoes, the uses of sunflowers, the dance language of bees and how it was discovered, the history and development of horses, and the economic, social, cultural, and religious life of a country. This lesson on Federalist Paper No. 10 is a content lesson. The students are not learning "how to"; rather they are learning the content

of Federalist 10. . . . *We have not developed a technology for practice in this type of lesson* [emphasis added]. (pp. 303–304)

Rosenshine's implied hope for a technology is representative of the reductionism so evident in educational thought. Educators want and seek the one answer or the one approach. Despite the cautions, one finds an assertion, as Rosenshine provided, that eventually researchers of teacher effectiveness will know enough to make all teachers deliver effective instruction in schools. The problem emerges when practitioners use the ideas of researchers to dictate a direction for instruction; when a research maxim is converted into a policy mandate. This can happen despite the intents of researchers or reformers. For example, those more inclined to the artistic dimension of teaching disdain mechanistic approaches. Indeed, some of the educational literature encourages the development of *reflectivity,* which would lead the teacher to think carefully and systematically about his or her actions; and *deliberateness,* which would lead the teacher to use the product of his or her reflection. This same literature is evolving now to what some school districts are describing as a *science of reflectivity.* Complex pedagogical propositions and ideas are made simple and treated as an emerging technology of reflectivity—as though reflection could be reduced to a technical skill!

Prospective teachers who understand the complexity of teaching would and should understand how and when to use explicit teaching or Hunter's (1983) instructional steps. They would understand how to apply a selected set of specific pedagogical principles. They would also understand, however, how to use other, more intuitive, teaching approaches (Parker, 1987) that defy reduction to a linear, delimited, step-by-step process. Teachers who have such an ability will be sources of innovation in schools (Hall, Doyle, & Hoffman, 1986) because they will appreciate the underlying dynamics of teaching and understand that intuition and artful judgment are important parts of effective practice and complements to technocratic skill. Such preservice teachers will be better equipped to cope with and challenge simplistic practices that treat teaching as a narrow, applied field.

Fourth Precondition: *Develop Curricular Cohesiveness Through Thematic Programming*

The curriculum of most teacher education institutions is not well integrated, nor is it designed to foster a schema for teaching. Faculty members create course objectives without consideration for larger curricular issues, and curriculum development similar to what Short (1987) espoused is uncommon, though most certainly it does on occasion occur (see Nolan, 1985).

Recently, educators have begun to discuss the need for unifying themes as part of the preservice teacher education. Zeichner's (1983) work on teacher education paradigms represented some of the first conceptual work on curricular alternatives for teacher education. He described four paradigms: behavioristic, personalistic, tradition-craft, and inquiry. Zeichner's work was definitionally weak, but subsequently researchers (see Tom, 1985) attempted to clarify the approaches, particularly the inquiry perspective. More recently, Gideonse (1986) discussed the notion of themes in his paper presented to the National Commission for Excellence in Teacher Education (e.g., teacher-as-artist, applied scientist, decision-maker, and moral craftsman). The organizing themes discussed by Gideonse were among the most prominently discussed in the literature of the early 1980s, though the terminology was often different than Zeichner's (e.g., Zeichner's behavioristic paradigm conceptually resembled Gideonse's teacher-as-applied scientist). The Gideonse themes were representative, not inclusive, of the total set of themes available. Indeed, as Short (1987) and Tom (1985) noted, the number of themes found implicitly or explicitly in the literature may be closer to 15 to 20. The power of the Gideonse work is the description of how a guiding image can strengthen and undergird teacher preparation programming. The lack of a common vision can prevent teacher-educators from realizing the goals they establish for programs.

Zeichner's and Gideonse's work provide philosophical rather than empirical support for thematic programming, showing that thematic teacher preparation enhances the educative nature of the curriculum. Theoretically, a guiding image should enhance the quality of a teacher education program. The work of cognitive psychologists (Shuell, 1986; Weinstein & Mayer, 1986) and schema theorists (Anderson & Smith, 1986) suggests that learning is inhibited not only when students fail to understand essential concepts but also when they fail to perceive the necessary interrelationships among those concepts. In teacher education, the question becomes whether it is imperative to develop and promote schemata or conceptual frameworks to help preservice teachers think about teaching. Barnes (1987) suggested that thematic preparation programs will be better in helping students deal with the complex decision-making associated with teaching.

Few empirical studies support Barnes' claim. Nonetheless, Barnes asserts that informal and formal data suggest that:

> Graduates of thematic programs are generally more satisfied with the quality of their programs than is true of alumni from the traditional program. One of the most important contrasts of this type centered on perceptions of the sources of professional knowledge. In a recent follow-

up study, graduates were asked to rate the extent to which their teacher education programs contribute to the development of their knowledge or competence in 15 different areas of teaching. . . . Relative to their counterparts in the Standard Program, graduates of thematic programs provided consistently higher ratings of program contributions across all areas of teaching cited in the survey. (p. 16)

Of course, thematic conceptual patterning is but one part of the overall effort to create curricular cohesiveness—other dimensions of programming, such as the policy-making and implementation phases (see Short, 1987), dictate whether the theme becomes a viable mechanism for helping preservice teachers make professional decisions.

Is there a best thematic direction for teacher education? Probably the answer is no, though some may be weaker or better than others in terms of fostering professional efficacy. For example, programs with a teacher-as-applied scientist theme may overemphasize skills, trivialize the teaching act, and contribute to anti-intellectualism (see Katz & Raths, 1985). Gideonse (1986) argued for a teacher-as-decision-maker theme, a thematic choice that emerges from his philosophical inclinations and personal dispositions about the roles and tasks of teachers.

The choice I would urge is to see teachers as decision makers. Teachers are required, hourly, to make serious value choices. They serve both individuals and society. They work in institutions where real power differentials exist. Their learning and teaching responsibilities are increasingly supported by an empirical research tradition requiring highly situational interpretation. (p. 192)

Most likely, there is no such thing as thematic *correctness* or *oughtness*. The efficacy of thematic curriculum-making is found in having most, though seldom all, faculty moving in the same direction. Such unity should not limit debate or deter dissent. What it will ensure is a collective sense of purpose and integration in the activities proffered within the curriculum. Certainly more research is needed to determine if this is true, but as Geertz noted, "you do not have to know everything to understand something."[1] Common sense suggests that an organization that moves in one direction will more likely achieve established goals than an institution that has many goals, purposes, and approaches. Although one might contend that open-endedness in teacher preparation

---

[1] Clifford Geertz, as quoted by Lee S. Shulman in audiotape "Educational Research Methodology—An Overview," produced by the American Educational Research Association.

leads to creativity and academic freedom for faculty, it also likely causes confusion and disorientation in students.

Perhaps for this reason few, if any, theorists writing on professionalism cite creative preparation practices as requisite for professional status. Indeed, most theorists cite the need for the acquisition of a specialized body of knowledge and the emergence of the behaviors and skills needed to put such knowledge into operation. These theorists may be thinking in a narrow manner. A better way to look at that specialized knowledge is to realize that it includes a wide range of skills and dispositions best learned in an environment that is unidirectional and focused. Instead of seeing the knowledge of effective teaching as distinct from a desire to practice it, teacher educators should see knowing and doing as linked together.

MISCONCEPTIONS OF TEACHER EDUCATION

The preconditions would suggest that change is both possible and necessary. Indeed they are ordered, to some extent, in terms of their complexity. The first precondition is a recognition of the need for an independent professional stance. To accomplish this, educators need to adjust their lexicon; the emphasis would no longer be on defining education through the use of comparisons, metaphorical or otherwise, with other professions. The second precondition is more difficult to achieve. It necessitates a shift in the responsibility for learning to the prospective teacher and away from the teacher educator. The third precondition requires a recognition of the dynamic and changing nature of the teaching act. And the final precondition necessitates a complete rethinking and reevaluation of the curriculum.

Developing a conceptual theme for teacher education programming is not a rhetorical exercise. Such change demands that program developers create a unified rather than a fragmented curriculum. Unfortunately, it is easier to maintain a fragmented curriculum than to develop a theoretically whole one. Fragmentation does not require intrafaculty dialogue, and it allows each faculty member to pursue his or her speciality without concern for the work of colleagues. Countering this tendency will not be accomplished easily. One illustration of how difficult intelligent integration may be is that all educators could agree to adopt a medical metaphor of teacher training and still end up teaching the same lessons they taught before they agreed to use the same image. A teacher-educator could frustrate integration by saying that what he or she teaches is part of the essential knowledge base and by ignoring how the skills or information he or she teaches is related to what a prospective teacher learns in other parts of a program or to the attitudes or values of a humane professional. The drive for integration means change should go beyond schools, colleges, and departments of education (SCDEs). Among the several implicit messages of the reform literature has been the notion that change cannot be limited to one segment of the educational community. All constituents must begin to evolve their programs to higher levels of sophistication and responsiveness.

The preconditions are necessary but not sufficient conditions for enhanced teacher education practice. They are first steps toward ensuring better teacher preparation experiences. By making unfair or unrealistic comparisons with other professions, we create assumptions that needlessly limit or improperly influence the training of prospective teachers. Or, by failing to develop a coherent conceptual basis for the teacher education curricula, we fail to provide preservice teachers with the necessary conceptual framework or schema they need to assimilate new ideas.

Unfortunately, three misconceptions militate against teacher-educators' fulfilling the aforementioned preconditions. The existence of one or more of these misconceptions prevents teacher-educators from realizing their own potential or from developing a curriculum that will have a positive impact on preservice teachers' skills for understanding teaching.

Misconception 1: *The Teacher Education Curriculum Must Be an Eclectic One*

This misconception is the result of a misunderstanding of pluralism and academic freedom. People think that when students are exposed to a variety of views and when teacher-educators are free to do what they want, the students will become well rounded and the teachers will pursue truth, wherever that chase leads them. Unfortunately, instead of the harmony consistent with a community of scholars, what results is chaos. The emphasis in the reform literature has been focused heavily on time questions: Are 4-year or 5-year programs best suited for preparing teachers? In the Holmes proposal and in the National Commission for Excellence in Teacher Education, much of the language is devoted to the need for 5-year programming (see Andrew, 1986; Holmes Group, 1986; Scannell, 1986). This emphasis is understandable given the political nature of the reform debate. But the main weakness with such proposals is that they extend teacher education and thereby potentially increase the fragmentation found in current programming efforts of teacher preparation. Tom (1987) described how intellectual and departmental divisions prevent ongoing dialogue between and among faculty:

Thus we often find departments of educational psychology, of curriculum and instruction, of social foundations, and so forth. These departmental divisions not only foster and legitimate the segmentation of the professional curriculum but also may actually physically separate the faculty holding different intellectual interests . . . by clustering the offices of faculty by department or by placing departments in different buildings. (p. 30)

In some ways, the fragmentation is caused by the way college professors are evaluated. The success of a faculty member is not based on teaching, most often, but rather on scholarship. This academic pursuit creates isolationism, because faculty work alone or in small groups on a specialized topic developing a research paper or article. Although such endeavors take time and are necessary for career advancement, they prevent the type of dialogue that fosters a unified curriculum. Nolan (1985) and others documented and described in detail how much work is involved and how much faculty time must be allocated if a truly unified curriculum is to be developed.

If research universities are to have primary responsibility for teacher education, an assertion evidenced throughout the Holmes proposal, then fragmentation in teacher education may well increase. The reason is simple: Faculty in research universities have been and will continue to be under more pressure to publish than are their colleagues in smaller teaching-oriented institutions.

Curriculum development takes time, requires tremendous amounts of faculty effort, and frequently has only modest payoffs. These realities perpetuate fragmented programming where, as Tom (1987) noted, an "assembly line" approach occurs, "with each professor adding a bolt or a fender to the prospective teacher" (p. 30). Assembly lines can do some things well, but teaching prospective teachers is not one of them.

[T]he professional curriculum does not necessarily add up to a completed "car"—not only because the professional curriculum lacks an overall design but also because each professor/worker sees only that part of [the] car which he or she is building. (Tom, 1987, p. 30)

To solve the problem of fragmentation, institutions do not need to establish 5-year programs. Rather, they need more curriculum development, more faculty cohesiveness, more faculty dialogue and team teaching, and enhanced organizational integratedness—the latter would enable faculty to see how the content of each course builds on the material taught in other professional education classes.

Misconception 2: *Every Teacher-Educator Must Be a Scholar*
Who Publishes Regularly in Professional Journals
This misconception results from the demands on teacher-educators being many and varied, perhaps more so than in the wider academic community. The expectations include what is called the real-world experience; a commitment to scholarly productivity; an ongoing awareness, at the very least, of what is happening in schools; and a dedication to service within and outside of the university community. The area of recent attention has been scholarship. The argument is that if teacher education is to be a part of academia, then teacher-educators must make a commitment to inquiry and scholarship (Ducharme, 1985; Ducharme & Agne, 1985).

The problem with the published-scholar assumption is that it reinforces faculty isolationism and causes many faculty to engage in activities that may ultimately be counterproductive to professional development—their own, or the profession's. The essential ingredient with regard to faculty scholarship is not publication but rather, as Wisniewski (1986) pointed out, professors who are active students of their craft: An individual who is active in his or her craft, understands the literature, can assimilate essential knowledge-based understandings found in the literature, and is able to apply those understandings to practical and theoretical problems.

Many exceptional teachers are poor writers or lack requisite research skills. And not all scholars are good teachers. The scholar-teacher is a rarity, at least when "scholar" is defined narrowly as one who demonstrates the capacity for research. Wisniewski's notion of an active student suggests a much broader perspective—an individual who is knowledgeable of state-of-the-art techniques and evidences veridicality in relations with others when working in the field. Such an individual understands how to critically read and apply research (preconditions two and three) so that it is a dynamic part of the teacher education curriculum, not an appendage to current course content.

At the same time, the relation of knowledge to professionalism is unclear. Throughout the literature on reform, one finds the term *knowledge base*. In *Educating a Profession*, Howsam et al. (1976) argued for the importance of the knowledge base for professional enhancement. More recently, Berliner (1985) called for inclusion in the preservice curriculum of knowledge for which there are no "counter indicators" (p. 4)—examples cited include Rowe's (1986) wait-time research and findings from the classroom management literature. The problem is this knowledge is almost pedestrian in content. A scholar most certainly should be aware of the knowledge base. He or she should be equally aware of its limits.

It is a strange and sad fact that even though the knowledge vis-à-vis teaching and teacher education has expanded during the past few decades, the knowledge is still highly fragmented and when used with educators it is treated in a reductionist fashion. Possession of certain truths will not make teachers more professional nor teacher education within the university curriculum more professionally efficacious, particularly if those truths are maxims about the need to wait for an answer after asking a question or the need to set clear rules in a classroom. Power and autonomy, not knowledge, per se, link professional training with universities (Judge, 1987). The relation of knowledge and status is important because it opens up the critical question of whether in professional schools one necessarily needs to contribute to the knowledge base in order to be called a scholar. The question is a difficult one that has been the focus of numerous polemics. Some scholars now envision role differentiation, with researchers and teachers assuming explicitly different roles in professional schools (Petersdorf, 1986). Researchers would not be expected to teach, though they would be able to deal with selected real-world problems; teachers would not need to conduct research, though they would be students of the available research. Such role differentiation is unappealing on one level (i.e., it may contribute to enhanced professional fragmentation). On another level, it may contribute to increased thought and harmony within a teacher education program, because all will be using the same general ideas but applying them according to their interests, desires, and abilities.

Misconception 3: *Teacher Education Is a Unidirectional Process, with Preservice Teachers Assuming Relatively Passive Roles*

Teacher-educators tend to impart a great deal of information in a short period of time; they tell the students what they need to know even before the students experience the need to know; they feed forward. Fortunately, enhanced field experiences challenge this misconception; preservice teachers are in schools more now as a regular part of their education. They are expected to observe and to reflect on what happens in schools and to engage in various forms of tutoring and teaching. In addition, in the calls of reformers, for example, the Holmes Group (1986) and the Carnegie Forum (1986), for radical new approaches to teaching teachers, one finds that the use of professional development centers will make preservice teachers even more active.

As pointed out earlier, one of the real problems with teacher education has been the limited impact that professional education experiences have on the values and beliefs of the matriculants. Students emerging from professional schools should be changed. Their essential under-standing of what it means to be a practicing professional should be different at graduation from what it was when they began the profes-sional curriculum. The comprehensiveness of the curriculum and the size of the teacher education program (i.e., the number of students) could prevent prospective teachers from experiencing the type of ed-ucative involvements they need to achieve a professional perspective in their thinking. With regard to curricular breadth, preservice curric-ulums may need to be structured along the lines of a less-is-more philosophy. Fewer ideas and skills would be covered, but more time would be spent developing the students' understandings and abilities.

Depth of curricular involvement for students is influenced by insti-tutional size. The difficulties in creating opportunities for close and intense student-faculty contact in large institutions and for identifying controlled school sites in which to develop students' pedagogical skills are enormous. Placing 50 practicum students is one thing; finding placements for 2,000 is quite another, to say nothing of training su-pervisors and ensuring that they accomplish with each student what is required.

There may be an inverse (or perhaps curvilinear) relationship between the size of the teacher education institution and the level of active involvement the preservice student has with curricular concepts and with faculty. Smaller and midsize institutions may be in a better position to engage students in critical dialogue about teaching skills and their use in lesson construction and implementation. Wait-time may become for students in larger schools an isolated skill that must be demonstrated to a campus supervisor, who may be an overloaded graduate student.

Interactive, reflective teacher education will be difficult to accomplish in extremely large, research-oriented institutions. This assertion is not empirically based, but it is grounded on the following assumption: Graduate students (who are often heavily involved in instruction at research universities) are not as knowledgeable as senior faculty and hence not as able to guide the instruction of prospective teachers to help them think deeply about what they need to do in a classroom to improve instruction. Further, graduate students (and part-time faculty) are not vested in preservice teacher development in the same manner as regular faculty.

As noted earlier, although teacher education research may best be accomplished at research universities, teacher education practice may best be achieved at teaching universities. Such institutions by definition are smaller and place a high value on student contact; they situate senior faculty in close proximity to preservice teachers. They limit the size of programs to ensure cohesiveness but are large enough to encourage diversity and to provide for varied interactions between and among students and faculty. Extremely small schools may be as ineffective as large ones. A certain critical mass of faculty is needed to offer effective programming. Certain types of faculty expertise are a precursor to appropriate program efforts. Perhaps, therefore, accreditation bodies should mandate parameters that limit both the smallness and largeness of an institution that prepares teachers.

MARKS OF IMPROVED TEACHER EDUCATION

Role differentiation on a broad scale may be needed for both faculty (some research, some teaching) and institutions (some research, some teaching). The danger here, as experts argue, is that role differentiation will lead to independent systems, which eventually seek to accomplish separate purposes (see, for example, Case, Lanier, & Miskel, 1986), but those same individuals assume a level of resources for education far in excess of what we currently have. They state, "It will cost money to achieve what can be done" (Case et al., 1986, p. 40). Yet financial support most likely will remain constant; it will not increase substantially. It is our view that financial constraints may be a benefit because educators will be forced to work collaboratively to improve their programs. They can accomplish the preconditions we outlined earlier, and they can effectively mitigate the power of the aforementioned misconceptions, by focusing on the following:

1. The institution makes a commitment to excellence: What the teacher education program does, it does well. This means the institution must look at what can best be accomplished given existing resources. As a result of this self-examination, the institution may choose not to provide a full range of programs. It may scale down in order to build up the quality of extant programming.
2. The institution engages in creative forms of cooperation with other colleges and universities (Kluender, 1986). In this way, the collective strength of several institutions overcomes any deficiencies evidenced in a particular school or college.
3. The faculty at an institution is willing to adjust its desire for personal advancement in order to enhance the overall programming efforts of the institution. This does not mean faculty are martyrs to the cause of teacher education, but neither are they a collection of prima donnas. The faculty and the administration recognize that they make the program, and it makes them. As a result, one finds a continual process of give and take, of individual surrender, and of collective reward.

4. The institution is of a size that enables a reasonable faculty-student ratio. Accrediting agencies should specify size parameters for professional schools that will enable not only appropriate faculty-student ratios but also ensure that economy-of-scale thinking does not supplant a reasonable perspective on the limits of teacher preparation programming.

Teacher education now finds itself at the crossroads. Maritain (1943) argued over 40 years ago that American education was bound by an instrumentalist and pragmatist philosophy that limited its capacity for inspiration and renewed power. Similarly, teacher education is bound by the traditions of past practice and by misconceptions engendered through the adoption of faulty metaphors that disguise compromise based on convenience rather than on the rigors of intelligent thought. Teacher education is threatened more by remaining on its current track than it is by outside critics who contend that teacher education is vacuous.

The road to inspired, powerful teacher education is one marked by new types of commitments. Those commitments will require teacher-educators to think more independently and clearly about the tasks they face. The commitments require giving up personal agendas for the broader betterment of the profession, relinquishing an ethos of faculty and institutional competitiveness for one marked by cooperation, and replacing program fragmentation with a more unified curricular direction that enables prospective teachers to think and act like professionals. The road is not a smooth one, but it is one that has the potential to lead teachers and teacher-educators to greater professional strength.

REFERENCES

Anderson, C.W., & Smith, E.H. (1986). *Children's conceptions of light and color: Understanding the role of unseen rays.* (Research services No. 166). East Lansing: Michigan State University, Institute for Research on Teaching.

Andrew, M.C. (1986). Restructuring teacher education: The University of New Hampshire's five-year program. In T.J. Lasley (Ed.), *The dynamics of change in teacher education* (pp. 59–87). (AACTE-ERIC Teacher Education Monograph No. 5). Washington, DC: American Association of Colleges for Teacher Education.

Barnes, H. (1987). The conceptual basis for thematic teacher education programs. *Journal of Teacher Education, 38*(4), 13–18.

Berliner, D. (1985). Laboratory settings and the study of teacher education. *Journal of Teacher Education, 36*(6), 2–8.

Bok, D. (1987, May-June). The challenge to schools of education. *Harvard Magazine,* pp. 47–79.

Buchmann, M. (1984). The use of research knowledge in teacher education and teaching. *American Journal of Education, 92,* 421–439.

Callahan, R.E. (1962). *Education and the cult of efficiency.* Chicago: University of Chicago Press.

Carnegie Forum on Education and the Economy. (1986). *A nation prepared: Teachers for the 21st century.* New York: Author.

Case, C.W., Lanier, J.E., & Miskel, C.G. (1986). The Holmes Group Report: Impetus for gaining professional status for teachers. *Journal of Teacher Education, 37*(4), 36–43.

Cheney, L. (1987). *American memory.* Washington, DC: National Endowment for the Humanities.

Ducharme, E.R. (1985). Establishing the place of teacher education in the university. *Journal of Teacher Education, 36*(4), 8–11.

Ducharme, E., & Agne, R. (1985). *The education professoriate: Towards scholastica.* Paper presented at the meeting of the American Educational Research Association, Chicago, IL.

Fenstermacher, G.D. (1987). On understanding the connection between classroom research and teacher change. *Theory into Practice, 26*(1), 3–7.

Gage, N. (1963). *Handbook of research on teaching.* Chicago: Rand McNally.

Gideonse, H.D. (1986). Guiding images for teaching and teacher education. In T.J. Lasley (Ed.), *The dynamics of change in teacher education* (pp. 187–197). (AACTE-ERIC Teacher Education Monograph (No. 5). Washington, DC: American Association of Colleges for Teacher Education.

Haberman, M. (1986). Licensing teachers: Lessons from other professions. *Phi Delta Kappan, 67*(100), 719–722.

Hall, G.E., Doyle, W., & Hoffman, J.V. (1986). The schools and preservice education: Expectations and reasonable solutions. In T.J. Lasley (Ed.), *The dynamics of change in teacher education* (pp. 19–27). (AACTE-ERIC Teacher Education Monograph No. 5). Washington, DC: American Association of Colleges for Teacher Education.

Holmes Group Executive Board (1986). *Tomorrow's teachers: A report of the Holmes group.* East Lansing, MI: Author.

Howsam, R.B., Corrigan, D.C., Denemark, G.W., & Nash, P.J. (1976). *Educating a profession.* Washington, DC: American Association of Colleges for Teacher Education.

Hunter, M. (1983). *Mastery teaching.* El Segundo, CA: TIP.

Jackson, P.W. (1987). Facing our ignorance. *Teachers College Record, 88*(3), 384–389.

Judge, H. (1987). Another view from abroad. *Teachers College Record, 88*(3), 394–399.

Katz, L., & Raths, J.D. (1985). Dispositions as goals for teacher education. *Teaching and Teacher Education, 1*(4), 301–308.

Kluender, M.M. (1986). The Nebraska consortium for improvement of teacher education. In T.J. Lasley (Ed.), *Issues in teacher education* (pp. 83–94). (AACTE-ERIC Teacher Education Monograph No. 6). Washington, DC: American Association of Colleges for Teacher Education.

Lasley, T.J. (Ed.). (1986a). *The dynamics of change in teacher education.* Washington, DC: American Association of Colleges for Teacher Education.

Lasley, T.J. (Ed.). (1986b). *Issues in teacher education.* Washington, DC: American Association of Colleges for Teacher Education.

Maritain, J. (1943). *Education at the crossroads.* New Haven, CT: Yale University Press.

National Education Association response: Status of the American public school teacher 1985–86. (1987). West Haven, CT: National Education Association.

Nolan, J.F. (1985). Findings from a case study. *Journal of Teacher Education, 36*(4), 12–16.

Parker, W.C. (1987). Teaching thinking: The pervasive approach. *Journal of Teacher Education, 38*(3), 50–56.

Petersdorf, R.G. (1986). Medical schools and research: Is the tail wagging the dog? *Daedalus, 115*(2), 99–118.

Rosenshine, B. (1987). Explicit teaching and teacher training. *Journal of Teacher Education, 38*(3), 34–38.

Ross, D.D., & Kyle, D.W. (1987). Helping preservice teachers learn to use teacher effectiveness research. *Journal of Teacher Education, 38*(2), 40–44.

Rowe, M.B. (1986). Wait-time: Slowing down may be a way of speeding up. *Journal of Teacher Education, 37*(1), 43–50.

Scannell, D. (1986). The University of Kansas extended teacher education program. In T.J. Lasley (Ed.), *The dynamics of change in teacher education* (pp. 89–99). (AACTE-ERIC Teacher Education Monograph No. 5). Washington, DC: American Association of Colleges for Teacher Education.

Short, E. (1987). Curriculum decision making in teacher education: Policies, program development, and design. *Journal of Teacher Education, 38*(4), 2–92.

Shuell, T.J. (1986). Cognitive conceptions of learning. *Review of Educational Research, 56*(4), 411–436.

Tom, A. (1985). Inquiring into inquiry-oriented teacher education. *Journal of Teacher Education, 36*(5), 35–45.

Tom, A. (1987). What are the fundamental problems in the professional education of teachers? In A. Wonsiewicz & M.J. Carbone (Eds.), *Excellence in teacher education through the liberal arts.* Allentown, PA: Muhlenberg College.

Wisniewski, R. (1986). The ideal professor of education. *Phi Delta Kappan, 68*(4), 288–292.

Weinstein, C.E., & Mayer, R.E. (1986). The teaching of learning strategies. In M.C. Wittrock (Ed.), *Handbook of research on teaching* (3rd ed., pp. 315–325). New York: MacMillan.

Zeichner, K. (1983). Alternative paradigms of teacher education. *Journal of Teacher Education, 34*(3), 3–18.

Chapter 2

Teacher Preparation in the Normal School*

R. S. Patterson

Dean, Faculty of Education
University of Alberta
Edmonton, Canada

The doors of Alberta's normal schools were closed in 1945, and teacher preparation for both elementary and secondary schools became an integral part of the university's program. This action distinguished Alberta as the first Canadian province to make all teacher preparation a responsibility of the university, and it also ended a period of 40 years wherein the normal schools were the main training ground for the province's teachers. In the years between 1906 and 1945, three different normal schools operated in Alberta. The first of these institutions opened in Calgary with an enrollment of 102 students. At their peak in the early 1940s, when wartime demand for teachers was excessive, the province's normal schools annually enrolled over 1,000 students who sought to gain their teaching certificates through the regular eight-month program or the abbreviated War Emergency plan, which required three months of study and practice. In this chapter, the work of these normal schools is examined and analyzed. It is hoped that the framework for analysis of these early teacher education institutions may be useful in examining contemporary and future provisions for teacher education.

It is one thing for the historian to outline the details of the past, including in the account such things as a chronology of main events, an outline of key participants and central ideas, and a description of

---

*The ideas central to this chapter were presented by the author in a conference on teacher education sponsored by the Centre for the Study of Teacher Education at the University of British Columbia in 1984.

human interrelationships, but it is far more interesting, challenging, and risky to provide an interpretative analysis of these data. In his book, *English Primary Education and the Progressives, 1914–1939,* Richard Selleck (1972) of Monash University illustrated part of this challenge through reference to an analogy. He claimed that an educational culture, such as that which we might associate with the normal schools and related public school phenomena, may be compared to the plotting and using of a map. He stated the following:

> In a map certain features from the multiplicity which any terrain possesses are organized according to conventions which make planning and prediction possible. Because the features are chosen with particular purposes in mind the same area can appear different on different maps—depending for example, on whether it was mapped to enable cars to drive easily through it, or to permit searches for oil to be begun, or battles to be fought. The use of a map (or the acceptance of an educational culture) means the limiting of an activity to a certain area; but it makes possible quick and efficient movement within that area. A person without a map may have unlimited freedom of choice, but often he may not know where to turn. Of course, a person who looks too long at one map may come to believe that the area he studies could be mapped in no other way, or he may even forget the existence of a whole world which is not contained on his map; so also an unreflecting acceptance of an educational culture may lead a teacher to believe that its customs and procedures are beyond criticism or the only possible way of acting.
> . . . the conditions of his profession give the teacher a great interest in the established procedures, the methods favored by his educational culture. By adopting them he is able to do the expected and so avoid criticism; they represent a means of reconciling the conflicting demands of the parties in the education process . . . they enable action to be taken without the anxiety and delay of calculating the consequences; they carry with them some assurance of success.
> . . . to attach the established procedures of an educational culture is to put a teacher's professional security at risk. (pp. 147–149)

For those involved in teacher education, especially those concerned with the examination of priorities, the revision of programs, or the allocation of resources, Selleck's analogy is useful. These people should ask the question, "To what extent are we locked into one way of viewing the world of education?" The established system has its own way of dealing with risk-takers, of thwarting innovations, or of discouraging changes that would disrupt and drastically alter the recognized way of doing things. For example, when admitting novices to the ranks of university or public school teaching, we tend to encourage and reward behaviors that perpetuate existing practice; we provide for probationary periods of service wherein the initiate is given the opportunity to demonstrate possession of the skills, attitudes, knowledge, and qualities of character requisite to meet accepted standards of successful performance. Only the very mature and secure, personally and institutionally speaking, or the indifferent and irresponsible are able to manifest uniqueness, variance, perhaps even radicalism, in relation to established patterns. The majority expect and are expected to follow the established map, the desire being, simply, to do it well. Deviance threatens the system, alters the map, and fosters acceptance of new rules and behavior. Those accustomed to the established order generally find such conduct disruptive, disfunctional, and even painful.

These considerations are important when writing history. Are events, people, and ideas to be described in relation to the ensconced viewpoint or are they to be used to plot a different schema for the same terrain? For instance, if we were to rely extensively on the existing map of our educational cultures, our histories of normal schools and teacher education probably would cover, in not too critical a fashion, the number of teachers prepared, the issues faced (such as preparing teachers for rural communities or for instruction at all grade levels or for new curricula), and the relationship of these developments to conditions elsewhere and to the personnel involved in the various activities. In Alberta, the Canadian focus of this study, we would speak of nearly 22,000 students who attended one of three institutions, Calgary, Camrose, and Edmonton, between 1906 and 1945. The significance of this number might be highlighted by comparing normal school attendance to university attendance and by observing that approximately one of every three people enrolling in formal postsecondary education in the first 40 years of Alberta's history attended a normal school. We might examine the career patterns of graduates and note how these individuals provided for the basic educational needs of thousands of young people in the public school system. Further, we could observe that many prominent influential educators in Alberta at one time attended normal school as a student and, not uncommonly, later served as a member of the faculty. University professors, government officials, school administrators, curriculum innovators, textbook authors, teachers, and members of other professions all include within their ranks numerous individuals who received a normal school education. The influence of the normal schools has been pervasive and, at the same time, it has been in harmony with maintaining the status quo. The curricula of the normal schools have stressed the importance of understanding the schools and of performing in them in a manner similar to that of contemporary school teacher practitioners. Faculty members who were chosen to instruct in the normal schools understood the school system and oriented prospective teachers accordingly. There was no encouragement offered to map the terrain differently. The cartographical changes to the educational map of the period were primarily additions and refinements, not efforts to achieve redesign and reconceptualization.

It should not be surprising that the histories of education and teacher education in Alberta tend to reflect the accepted educational map. They do not challenge the preferred mode of viewing and analyzing the system. Some commentators may offer negative views on the features of a curriculum or question the appropriateness of a methodology or fault an administrative structure, but essentially such is done within the accepted framework, thus offering little more than suggestion for a modest tinkering with the system. In reference to Selleck's map analogy, these comments may be likened to deciding which roads to plot on a road map. They do not propose an alternative use for the map nor a representation of entirely different information. Implicit in the way that the majority of us views the educational enterprise of which we are a part is the belief that what has transpired and is occurring in education, including teacher education, has been and continues to be, for the greater part, worthwhile and valuable. To entertain the opposite perspective is to promote denial from those who are not prepared to believe otherwise or frustration in those who agree but who see no way to change things long established and reinforced by tradition, practice, and organizational structure. To seriously criticize the existing map and to propose a major change is, in the eyes of some observers, akin to denigrating or depreciating the actions, motives, and intelligence of well-intentioned, caring, industrious, able people. When one looks back and notes the remarkable sacrifices made by teachers in the face of real adversity as they contended with the problems of the one-room country school, including isolation, overcrowding, overwork, diverse ethnic and language backgrounds, limited motivation for schooling, and instruction in multiple grades, it takes considerable courage, gall, or stupidity to even query whether or not these teacher contributions were anything less than significant and infinitely valuable. Many of us, as we review where we have been and where we are, regard our position positively and optimistically. We are inclined to think of our society in terms of progress, advancement, and achievement. We see in our society advances in science, technology, and medicine, reduction of work, increasing affirmation of human rights, improved access to education, improved levels of literacy and school-grade attainment, and we arrive at the conclusion that ours is a record of significant accomplishment in overcoming major problems, challenges, and handicaps. In the educational arena, we point to such indicators of success as high-quality school buildings, relatively low teacher/pupil ratios, near-perfect literacy levels, expanding, varied school services, number of diploma or degree recipients, and the wide range of clientele served as the basis for defending the belief that our educational provisions are not only adequate but, even better, they are well developed and highly beneficial. It is important to recognize that although these characteristics of our educational system legitimately may serve as indicators of our commitment to and interest in schooling, it does not follow necessarily that size, expense, variety, modernity, elaborateness, and numbers are sufficient, adequate, or appropriate gauges of success and achievement when it comes to evaluating the quality of educational experiences. They may be the features currently plotted on our educational map, but perhaps we would be benefited by asking whether or not other information would be more pertinent and helpful as the focal point of attention in assessing our educational growth and accomplishment.

Consider, as the basis of an alternative perspective for judging what has been accomplished in public education and teacher preparation, some of the ideas of John Dewey. In describing approaches to preparing teachers, he identified two basic alternatives, the apprenticeship and the laboratory models, of which he clearly preferred the latter. Arthur G. Wirth (1966) outlined the views of Dewey on these two models of teacher education in his book *John Dewey as Educator: His Design for Work in Education (1894–1904)*. The common meanings of these two terms capture the essential elements of Dewey's distinction as described by Wirth. Apprenticeship implies imitation of model behavior, mastery of essential skills, and acceptance of routine procedures as the basis of action. In contrast, the laboratory approach is seen to involve problem identification, intelligent judgment, and imaginative application of knowledge with appropriate ensuing analysis and evaluation, the results of which influence subsequent behavior. For Dewey, the laboratory model was essentially a continuous growth model. Teachers so prepared were to acquire the skills, knowledge, and attitudes that would enable and incline them to continue learning about teaching throughout their careers. In short, they would become permanent students with their classroom as their laboratory. Although the apprenticeship model is not seen to have the advantages associated with producing individuals disposed to relate critically and experimentally to the challenges of teaching, it is not without its compensating virtues and appeal. Foremost among these is that, generally, teachers prepared in this way possess the skills and knowledge sufficient to provide acceptable service as a novice teacher; that is, they are able to manage a classroom effectively by keeping order, following an orderly plan of instruction, and measuring and evaluating student achievement. In supporting a different conception of acceptable teacher performance, Dewey did not belittle or ridicule either the pressure for beginning practitioners to have apprenticeship skills or the well-intentioned efforts to provide them. He recognized the obvious demands of the classroom on both the novice and the experienced teacher. He believed, however, that to focus teacher preparation primarily on skill mastery and the learning of behaviors and attitudes designed to facilitate accommodation to the established system at the expense of the development of an approach to teaching that encouraged experimentation, weighing of alternatives, critical examination of performance, and continuous pursuit of knowledge relevant to the nature of the learner and to an understanding of subject matter was to adopt a myopic view of teaching that sacrificed long-term benefits for immediate, instrumental gain. Dewey advocated a form of teacher preparation that would foster the acquisition of insights and an approach to teaching designed to encourage continuous professional growth. He believed that if these are not obtained in preservice preparation, they are difficult to acquire later, whereas increased proficiency in technical skill development and mastery is something more readily acquired on the job. Even more important to his scheme of things was the viewpoint that emphasis on attaining proficiency in teaching skills tends to divert the attention of the student teacher toward less significant concerns, thereby discouraging participation in more positive, worthwhile learning experiences.

In discussing the behavior of learners, Dewey (1904) distinguished between external and internal levels of learning. He pointed out that most students learn to evince signs indicating attention, interest, or understanding. By nodding the head in obvious agreement or by smiling at an appropriate moment, we lead the teacher-observer to believe we are listening and learning. Although we rely on these external signs in our interaction, they are not reliable indicators of what the individual is learning. It is relatively easy to disguise our interest. Dewey wanted teachers to address internal levels of learning, as he believed the real challenge of teaching consists of recognizing and influencing the mind activity of students. He (Dewey, 1904, p. 8) warned against those individuals who "seem to know how to teach," but who "are not students of teaching." He felt that even though such teachers go about

studying books of pedagogy, reading teachers' journals, attending teachers' institutes, etc., yet the root of the matter is not in them, unless they continue to be students of subject matter and students of mind activity. Unless a teacher is such a student, he may continue to improve in the mechanics of school-management but he cannot grow as a teacher, an inspirer and a director of soul-life. (p. 8)

Dewey did not view teaching as a technical enterprise, although performance skills are a part of the activity. Along with the importance of having teachers who are students of mind activity, he stressed the need to have teachers "who have been taught to see their subject matter as a product of thought in action, who understand the disciplines that led to the advance of knowledge as well as the end products in textbooks" (p. 17). He advocated the need to have teachers "who are themselves so full of the spirit of inquiry, so sensitive to every sign of its presence and absence, that no matter what they do, nor how they do it, they succeed in awakening and inspiring like alert and mental activity in those with whom they come in contact" (p. 17).

The foregoing ideas from Selleck and Dewey have been introduced as a framework for a critical review of the history of teacher education in the normal schools of Alberta. They may be useful for a similar analysis in other provinces, states, or countries. The map analogy raises questions about the purposes of the teacher education enterprise and the most appropriate indicators for study in determining whether or not these purposes have been realized. It opens up the value of shifting our perspective and of challenging the conventional evaluative criteria. Dewey's views of a laboratory model of teaching and of internal and external levels of learning have relevance to judging individual learning performance, but they also open up ways of reflecting on societal developments. One application would be to ask whether or not we are looking at internal or external signs of learning when we judge our educational systems by growth in per capita expenditure for education or number of diplomas awarded. It would seem consistent with Dewey's position to suggest that we need to examine what members of our society do with the education received. This implies the use of a different set of evaluative standards in contrast to those currently in vogue.

Perhaps it is unreasonable to expect anything more of the normal schools than the acceptance of the apprenticeship model. If, however, the universities in their approach to teacher education accept or endorse a similar approach, then there is serious reason to question the placement of teacher preparation in universities and the claim that our educational system is offering learners an adequate fare. The more schools and colleges of education and universities succumb to the pressure to prepare people for specific employment opportunities as identified and described by future employers, the more reason we have to doubt that these institutions are offering a type of education designed to foster continuous learning on the part of their graduates.

An examination of the nature of teacher education provided in the normal schools is useful in that it offers insight into the educational map employed over nearly 50 years of Alberta's history. In fact, it may provide the key to understanding our complete educational history insofar as subsequent teacher education is little more than an extension of earlier practice. Two hypotheses are worth exploring in relation to this theme:

1. Teacher education in the normal school era highlighted an apprenticeship model of teaching with the attendant result that teacher education perpetuated the use of the existing educational map and resulted in a gradual decline in intellectual activity in our society.
2. Reference to a set of evaluative criteria that is not an accurate indicator of educational growth for individuals or society has contributed to an ill-founded belief in our educational advancement. Attention to criteria that gauge external signs of commitment and interest obscures examination of the important questions as to what people are learning and what they are doing with their learning.

By producing generations of "safe," acceptable teachers, ones who are familiar with the established order and who are able through their skill mastery to fit comfortably into it, the normal schools have done a disservice to our society, because through these teachers they have, unwittingly, undermined the quality of intellectual activity described by Dewey that should be the trademark of a progressive, free society.

Four facets of the normal school teacher preparation program are referred to in this historical account. These include:

1. the nature of the normal school curriculum,
2. the characteristics of the student body,
3. relationships between and among the various partners in the teacher preparation program, and
4. the roles and responsibilities of the normal school faculty.

Of the four topics, the first two, the curriculum and the students, receive the most attention in the reported observations and comments of the normal school principals of the period. In the early years, before 1918, when an eight-month period of preparation was introduced as the basic requirement for all normal school programs, considerable concern was voiced over the limitations imposed by the shorter four-month term. An examination of both the curriculum of the four-month training program and the criticisms directed at it provides fundamental insight into the view of the teacher that was dominant in the period. Dr. Coffin, a Calgary Normal School principal, noted that there was not enough time to deal with the subject matter preparation of the students, with the result that their methodological skills suffered *(Annual Report of the Department of Education,* 1914, p. 30). Instruction in the wide range of school subjects, including agriculture, school gardening, domestic science, manual training, and domestic art, could do little more than give prospective teachers a grasp of the place of these subjects in the public school curriculum. The advantages acknowledged in the 8-month course by Mr. Stickle, the principal at Camrose Normal in 1919, indicate that even the extension of the training period did not drastically alter the established nature of teacher preparation. Stickle spoke of the chance to help students form proper habits of study, to review the public school curriculum from the teacher's standpoint, to provide for more observation and practice in the classroom, to offer more first-hand knowledge of rural school conditions and methods, to illustrate theories, to provide additional courses, and to study problems of organization and administration by observation and experiment (pp. 43–44). The main concern, even after the introduction of the eight-month course, remained one of orienting teachers to the system. There was no sign of a concern to offer them a basis for critically evaluating the educational order. Students, according to Dr. Coffin, were unable or uninclined to develop a dynamic rather than a static knowledge of subject matter (p. 31). This meant that their interest in subject matter was limited to knowing enough to teach the content of the curriculum. Subsequent normal school program revisions fail to offer evidence to support the belief that Coffin's concern precipitated curriculum modifications to address this deficiency. Such a change, had it occurred, would have moved teaching and teacher education toward a new, more vital educational purpose. The era between 1936 and 1945 in Alberta, when a group of reformers heralded and endorsed the merits of progressive education, offered the opportunity for a major overhaul of schooling and teacher preparation. Such change was not forthcoming. The pressures exerted by hiring authorities, inspectors, superintendents, teachers, and parents discouraged the full adoption of the new educational perspective. Teachers lacked an appreciation of the philosophy undergirding the reform and, in the main, encouraged a return to a curriculum and methodology in keeping with established practice. The failure to grasp and to implement the new theory reinforces the claim that teachers lacked in their preparation the type of education essential to change and advancement.

Throughout the history of the normal schools, one element of the program received more attention than any other. Observation and practice was constantly discussed, not with the view of opening up new insights into the school experience, nor of stimulating a spirit of enquiry and experimentation on the part of teachers, nor of encouraging teachers to be students of mind activity and of subject matter. One of the chief administrators of the program observed in 1920 that "practice teaching is, of course, the *sine qua non* of the course whatever else has to be omitted or condensed" *(Annual Report,* 1914, p. 51). A decade later Dr. Haverstock, the Camrose Normal School principal, attempted to place practice teaching in perspective in relation to the rest of the programs. It was his view that, although the normal school personnel did not wish to minimize in any way the value or importance placed on practice teaching, they felt that

> . . . students come to our institutions with erroneous ideas as to the importance of practice teaching. It is a factor in determining an individual's fitness to enter the teaching profession, but it is not by any means the only factor. A student, in addition to making a good showing in practice teaching, must be able to apply himself from day to day to the routine work of the school. (p. 27)

Although Haverstock attempted to reduce the emphasis on practice teaching, he still put forth a view of teacher preparation based on imitation of existing practice and accommodation to the system. The continuing plea for rural school experience in the program reflected the same belief that teacher preparation required opportunities to participate in experiences identical to those of the practicing teacher.

The extracurricular element of the normal school program also played an important part in the socialization of prospective teachers. Included in this were such activities as picnics, drama presentations, musicals, athletic competitions, school government, publications, and parties and dances. The value of these activities should not be minimized or underestimated, for they afforded the faculty another means of equipping prospective teachers with values, attitudes, and skills appropriate to their future role in society. They also left students with a positive feeling toward their teachers and their career preparation that, undoubtedly, in turn increased the likelihood that these fledgling teachers would act as expected. Contemporary teacher educators could learn much from the way normal school instructors utilized the total program of the institution to instill attitudes and values that were vital to the future teaching performance of the graduates. The beginning normal school graduates may not have been well equipped as far as their knowledge of teaching, but they were well imbued with values focused on a commitment to serving students.

There were those who challenged the traditional view of teacher preparation. In a major report, *The Training and Certification of Teachers for Alberta Schools,* written in 1936, H. C. Newland asserted that "the curriculum is too exclusively technical, even for a one-year course" (p. 32). Little was changed despite the criticism. Thus, in relation to the nature of the normal school program and its effect on teachers and public school experience, it seems reasonable to conclude that the normal school program

1. was designed in purpose, method, and content to prepare a group of teachers who understood, accepted, and followed, unconditionally, the established educational map. There was a curriculum to master and to teach, a method to be used, and an order to be maintained;
2. included extracurricular activities that not only developed or en-hanced useful creative, artistic, or physical abilities but that also (and more importantly) helped the students feel positive about their training and inclined them to adopt similar practices, even under adverse circumstances, in their classrooms and schools;
3. did not encourage or facilitate intellectual enquiry. Instead, it em-phasized adoption of relatively standardized, repetitive procedures that discouraged prospective teachers from finding the excitement and challenge of investigating questions about content or learning that would enable them to promote similar experiences with their students.

It appears that the society wanted technician teachers, and the normal schools provided them. To accept this is to acknowledge a related deleterious effect on public schooling. Gradually, but surely, the per-petuation of such a system of preparing teachers helped to undermine the hope that children in the public schools, in the main, would have stimulating, exciting learning experiences.

The nature of the student body attending normal schools also con-tributed to the growth of a teaching force not inclined or able to provide classroom instruction directed at provoking enquiry and investigation. The normal schools did not attract students who, by virtue of ability, educational achievement, or social standing, sought to confront and disrupt the established order. There is reason to believe that for most of the years of their existence, the normal schools attracted reasonably intelligent females and less talented and less able male candidates. Not uncommonly, the shortage of males was decried, mainly because they were viewed as prime candidates for administrative positions. Despite their obvious strength in numbers and ability, the women did little to challenge this obvious prejudice. The ability of normal school students was a common target of criticism and abuse throughout the history of these institutions, except, perhaps, during the 1930s when a surfeit of teachers helped to maintain higher admission standards. Times of teacher shortage were sufficiently frequent and common, however, to warrant repeated adoption of the expedient measure of lower admission requirements. The observation of one Department of Education official in a letter to an American educator captures the essence of the condition. It was his opinion that the normal school students were "not the ablest of the high school population" (Newland, 1942, p. 1). Statements and observations made by normal school principals in their annual reports reinforce this description of the student body. These leaders often spoke of student immaturity, poor academic qualifications, and deteriorating quality in the ability of students. This same point was made by reference to the large number of rural students attending normal schools. It was generally recognized that rural school education was inferior to that of the urban areas. Also, it was known that the majority of students in the normal schools was from the rural area. For instance, it was noted in 1937–38 that 64% of the student body was from farm homes, with this number rising to 80% in 1943–44 *(Annual Report,* 1943, p. 41). Dr. McDougall (1946), in commenting on the effect of rural student enrollment, noted that

> the rural student has received his elementary and much of his secondary education in the weakest element of the Alberta educational system. Though they are the inheritors of many of the deficiencies which accrue to the graduates of such schools, yet these former students return as teachers to perpetuate in the living of others the same influences which make their own living narrow and incomplete. (p. 11)

Just as in the case of female students, where the ability level was high but the inclination to challenge the system was low, so, too, the prominence of certain ethnic and religious groups tended to reflect similar conditions. These groups saw teacher education as an avenue for gaining social acceptance and mobility. Their disproportionate enrollment in normal school may also have been an indicator of their inability to find better alternatives, especially in the difficult financial times of the Depression. In the 1930s, at least one fifth of the enrollment of the Edmonton Normal School was of Ukrainian descent (Deverell, 1946, p. 61). This may well have been a selective population as far as ability, thus questioning the view that the normal school students were intellectually weak. At the same time, this group of ethnic minorities, being a population eager to find social acceptance, provides strong support to the view that these candidates, like many others of their fellow students, were inclined not to question the system or the established mode of teaching. The combined effect of ability level, coupled with the social and economic opportunities available to the rural populace, women, and members of religious and ethnic minorities, ensured that the bulk of the normal school students would endorse and perpetuate a view of teaching that would not accentuate critical scholarship or intellectual inquiry. The plea of one inspector for students with "the three G's of success, Go, Grit and Gumption" *(Annual Report,* 1907, p. 48), indicates a widespread absence of characteristics in teachers that would improve or uplift the quality of educational experience.

A third facet of the normal schools that, because of its nature, did not alter the existing educational map was that of the partnership among teacher educators in the normal schools, the public schools, and the Department of Education. Participants from all three spheres of the partnership maintained a close working relationship and reinforced a commonly held view of teaching and teacher preparation. Several factors contributed to this accord. Because the staff of the normal schools were employees of the Department of Education, male personnel moved easily between positions on the faculty and on the inspection staff. A large percentage of senior civil servants in the Department served at one time on the faculty of a normal school. The link with teachers in the classroom came through visits to schools to observe practice teachers, joint participation in conventions and institutes, and shared visits with members of the inspection staff. Teachers, often former normal school students in Alberta, seemed willing and eager to help in providing practice facilities for student teachers, even when in years of heavy enrollments the numbers placed excessive demands on them. In part, this response was attributable to the favorable relationship established between these teachers and the normal school faculty when these teachers were their students. The normal school staff evidenced its interest in keeping in touch with the classroom by participating in annual extended visits with school inspectors. The implication of this close association with classroom teachers is that the normal school staff was inclined, on the basis of this experience, to direct the learning of students toward accepted practice. Emphasis was placed, accordingly, on practical training, imitation and repetition, and mastery of accepted skills and techniques that related to the existing order. The harmony and liaison among the teacher education partners of the day encouraged the development of a common perspective. Their cooperation, oriented as it was to a field-based perspective, meant that new teachers were not equipped with an approach to learning and teaching that would foster a spirit of enquiry and restructuring. Given the view of teaching and teacher preparation of the period, it is not difficult to understand why the partners in teacher education enjoyed harmonious relations. By failing to confront and threaten the established view of things and, instead, by endorsing the commonly held orientation, the normal school faculty ensured that teacher education would remain safe.

The final area to consider in looking at the normal school view of teaching is that of the role and responsibility of the faculty itself. These people provided the model for the students. However, their example did not represent an appropriate ideal, at least not to Dr. Coffin who, in 1926, made the following observation:

> With individual or group conferences, participation in or supervision of student activities, ordinary preparation of class work, and reading of assigned reports, essays and examination papers, both regular and supplemental, an instructor has no difficulty in finding his or her time fully occupied, not to speak of the need of keeping somewhat in the wake of educational progress through reading. Educational research and experimentation are almost out of the range of possibility. And yet a Provincial Normal School ought to be a centre of educational enquiry and outlook, and not merely a piece of educational mechanism for the supply of current needs. *(Annual Report, 1907, p. 24)*

In addition to facing the demands associated with heavy teaching loads, the normal school faculty was involved in a multiplicity of other activities, including attending teacher institutes and conventions, adjudicating school fairs, evaluating practice teaching, preparing professional examinations for teachers, visiting rural schools, revising curricula, publishing articles, teaching summer school, and pursuing graduate studies, all of which left little or no time for these people to provide educational leadership or to be proper role models actively involved in the study of education. So heavy was the teaching load in the 1930s that enrollment quotas were introduced to protect against faculty overload. Dr. Coffin saw the importance of the normal schools providing leadership, not through an endless array of activities related to the field and instruction, but instead through research, experimentation, and publication. So busy were these teacher educators in responding to the demand for teachers, so eager were they to provide more graduates who through preservice or inservice activities would fit comfortably into the system, that they had little or no time to evaluate the effect of their performance, to engage in critical scholarship relative to the accepted traditions of the day, or to offer alternatives to assured accommodation to the system.

There were some students who managed to acquire a perspective on learning and teaching in harmony with the one associated with Dewey and outlined in this chapter. For example, one student recounted how his experience with Dr. Dickie, a long-time female staff member at both Camrose and Edmonton, gave him a lifelong appreciation of literature, one he tried to share with students and family. He spoke of Sunday evening group discussions in her home where he was introduced to the joy of good literature. He described his experience as follows:

> She introduced me to *Anne of Green Gables.* "I realize that it is primarily a girl's book, Mr. Hornby. But now that winter is here and you can't play soccer, I think it would do you good to meet Anne Shirley." And I have always been glad I did. I buy copies of the series for my grandchildren. She introduced me to Shaw (Major Barbara), Oscar Wilde (The Importance of Being Earnest) and Sheridan (The Rivals). She used to assign parts to each of us, she always had enough copies and we would read aloud—an enjoyable learning experience. . . . [Once] she read Marjorie Pickthall's short poem, "The Shepherd Boy." She read it twice. . . . After this she took a volume of Milton's poems and discussed "Samsom Agonistes," his memories, remorse and despair . . . I have never been so moved by a poem. (Hornby, n.d., p. 3)

The experience vividly illustrates the type of learning a teacher should strive to produce, the type that most students missed, the type Mr. Hornby would have missed had he not been a member of Miss Dickie's extracurricular Sunday afternoon tea group. This was not the common offering or outcome of the normal school curriculum.

The viewpoint shared within this chapter is in harmony with the observations of Zeichner and Tabachnick (1981, pp. 7–10) on the effects of teacher education. They examined the generally accepted phenomenon of students adopting progressive or liberal attitudes during their university studies and then shifting to more traditional views as they commence teaching. One explanation posited is that the universities are essentially conservative in their effect, for they fail to offer students "conceptual tools which would enable them to transcend the structural contexts within which teaching and learning currently occur" (p. 9). The authors suggested that the underlying message of the university to conform prevents "analytical and autonomous teaching from becoming a reality" (p. 9) Certainly, the normal school experience described in this chapter served to have a similar effect on our teacher candidates of an earlier era.

. There is reason to believe that the observations made in this chapter have some relevance to the activity of determining priorities and future directions in schools, colleges, and faculties of education. Reference to alternative ways of examining the educational map and the attempt to provide a different view of our past have been made in order to provoke thought about what has been and is being done in teacher education. An ideal, one based on John Dewey's analysis, has been suggested. It is an ideal that should be in harmony with the concepts of university and education. The position advanced through this historical glance is that teacher education, at any level, preservice, continuing, and graduate, should be of such a nature as to ensure that those participating as students will be led to pursue and enjoy the challenge, the excitement, and the fulfillment of enquiry whether related to the mind activity of students or the discipline of content areas. Those who are so taught will, in turn, provide comparable learning experiences for their students. To initiate people to the fraternity of learning excitement, teachers themselves must belong.

There is a tendency to direct undergraduate and graduate teacher education programs to the perceived needs and conditions of the classroom and to measure their value in instrumental terms. The result is the preparation of teachers, administrators, and other personnel who fail to provide critical analysis of schooling. Instead, their creativity, imagination, and intelligence, to the extent that they are developed and/or utilized, make modifications to existing practice that do not alter, fundamentally, the structure and values of the system. To fail, as did the normal schools, to stress, to seek, and to provide for teaching and teachers characterized by an interest in and a commitment to the furtherance of knowledge through a spirit of enquiry, investigation, and evaluation, is to ensure the continued depreciation of the pursuit.

The time has come in teacher education to reexamine our educational map. We need to shift our orientation and avoid the temptation of continuing to use irrelevant data to assess our contribution. The technology we use, the distance we cover, the jobs filled by our graduates, the number of courses we offer, the range of services provided, and the size of our faculty and our enrollments are not adequate gauges of our performance. To plot and use these data on our map is to guarantee the continued pursuit of goals somewhat removed from those identified in this chapter. It may be that many believe we endorse and pursue the ideals enunciated here. If such is the case, then the task before us is one of ensuring that our faculty and our students participate in the venture in such a way that our collective behavior attests to the fact. At present, it would seem that although our programs are much longer and varied in nature than those of the normal school, the overall impact of contemporary teacher preparation is akin to that of our normal schools. As yet, we have some distance to travel; we certainly need to consider the features to be identified on our educational map that will help us evaluate our progress toward our destination; we may even need to determine whether or not our goal is readily apparent and generally accepted.

REFERENCES

Annual report of the department of education. (1907). Alberta, Canada: King's Printer.
Annual report of the department of education. (1914). Alberta, Canada: King's Printer.

Annual report of the department of education. (1943). Alberta, Canada: King's Printer.

Deverell, J.M. (1946). *The Ukrainian teacher as an agent of cultural assimilation.* Unpublished master's thesis, University of Toronto.

Dewey, J. (1904). The relation of theory to practice in education. In National Society for the Scientific Study of Education, *Third yearbook,* Part 1.

Hornby, J.B. (n.d.). Questionnaire response #302. *Project yesteryear files.* Alberta, Canada: University of Alberta.

McDougall, W.D. (1946). *Suggestions for the improvement of elementary teacher education in the province of Alberta.* Unpublished doctoral project, Teachers College, Columbia University, New York.

Newland, H.C. (1936, June 24). The training and certification of teachers for Alberta schools. In W. Aberhart (Ed.), *Minister of education papers* (pp. 20–21). Province of Alberta Archives.

Selleck, R.J.W. (1972). *English primary education and the progressives, 1914–1939.* London: Routledge & Kegan Paul.

Wirth, A.G. (1966). *John Dewey as educator: His design for work in education (1894–1904).* New York: John Wiley & Sons, Inc.

Zeichner, K., & Tabachnick, B. R. (1981), Are the effects of university teacher education "washed out" by school experience. *Journal of Teacher Education, XXXII*(3), 7.1.

Chapter 3

A Plight of Teacher Educators: Clinical Mentalities in a Scientific Culture*

James Raths

University of Vermont

Amy McAninch
Lilian Katz

University of Illinois at Urbana-Champaign

INTRODUCTION

C. P. Snow (1959) wrote convincingly of the existence of two cultures within the university community—that of science and that of humanities. However, university communities are decidedly not bicultural in their orientations, but multicultural. Many more than two cultures coexist in every university setting. University faculty primarily engaged in training functions, including teacher educators, have come to know and appreciate two particular cultures that are endemic to the university community and that are profoundly influential in their lives (Kimble, 1984; Sergiovanni, 1985). One of these cultures is associated with the world of the researcher, the scientist, who seeks to understand and generate new knowledge. The second has to do with the arena of the

* This chapter originally appeared in a slightly different form in Wisniewski R., & Ducharme E. (Eds.). (1989). *The Professors of Teaching: An Inquiry* (pp. 105-118). New York: State University of New York Press.

practitioner, the trainer, the developer, who applies knowledge to complex and demanding individual cases and in turn trains others to do the same.

This chapter focuses on the impacts of the clash between these two cultures on the lives of teacher educators, recognizing that many others within the university community are affected by it. Subcultures coexist in many locations within the university. As Dearden (1983) reminded us:

. . . the relation between theory and practice causes puzzlement across a very wide field. How is economics related to running a business, jurisprudence to being a lawyer, theology to faith, ethics to conduct, logic to reasoning, or, for that matter, sociology to being a police inspector? (p. 5)

As we shall see, these two coexisting worlds are quite disparate. Schwab (1978), in inquiring into these distinctions (but with different rubrics), asserted:

The radical difference of the practical from the theoretic mode is visible in the fact that it differs from the theoretic not in one aspect but in many: It differs from the theoretic in method. Its problems originate from a different source. Its subject matter is of a distinctly different character. Its outcome is of a different kind. (p. 288)

In short, the cultures have different folkways, accept different values, address different challenges, and require different mentalities on the part of their actors. Of course, both realms are critical to the functioning of the university as a locus of efforts to carry out research, service, and teaching, but their mutual commitment to the ends advanced by the university does not diminish the tensions that exist between members of the two groups.

Freidson (1972) documented the existence of this particular cultural division of the university community in his study of the sociology of the medical profession. Freidson suggested that medical practitioners have a different orientation to their work than medical researchers. In fact, Freidson asserted that this disparity in mindset extends well beyond the world of work and is manifested in contrasting views of the world. In sum, persons devoted to practice think differently about problems, have different norms, and use different problem-solving patterns than do those who are committed primarily to research.

Clinical mentality and *scientific mentality* are not normative terms.[1] In our culture, the values ascribed to almost anything labeled scientific suggest that the clinical label may have derogatory connotations. That is not the thrust of Freidson's work, nor of this chapter. The terms are meant to be descriptive and neutral.

Our descriptions of the major attributes of the clinical and scientific mentalities are based on extrapolations from Freidson's work. We close with some implications our analysis holds for the organization and administration of teacher education.

CONTRASTING CLINICAL AND SCIENTIFIC MENTALITIES

There are at least five attributes that, according to Freidson, differentiate clinical and scientific mentalities. The attributes include readiness to act, confidence, source of justifications, search for knowledge, and uses of knowledge. Each of these attributes, summarized in Table 1, is discussed below.

Readiness to Act
Individuals with clinical mentalities feel compelled to act when faced with a problem or a demanding client. They are unlikely to study the problem further, to collect more data, to read up on the peculiarities of a particular case. Instead, it is seen as important to do something, to try something, to intervene. Individuals with scientific mentalities, in contrast, almost always resist rushing into action, holding that reflective and deliberate thought is the proper response before acting in a problematic situation. Thus, researchers tend to review the alternatives for action, explore each option's indicators and counterindicators, and consult with others before acting. Thus, the penchant to act versus the tendency to deliberate differentiates the clinical mentality from the scientific.

---

[1] Several critics of earlier drafts of this chapter have called us to task for using the term *mentality* to describe teacher educators' orientation to their work. A number of our colleagues felt it had a negative and pejorative connotation, as though mentalities were normally thought to be negative, or that having a mentality in and of itself suggests that the teacher educator in question is somehow less of a person, is an individual out of control, or in the throes of some sort of spell. As we have made plain, our essay is based firmly on the work of E. Freidson (1972), and it seems important for us to use his term in order to properly acknowledge his contribution to our thinking. Of course, Professor Freidson bears no responsibility for the interpretations we have made of his writing.

TABLE 1. Principal Attributes of the Scientific and Clinical Mentalities

Attribute	Scientific	Clinical
Readiness to act	Inclined to seek more information before acting	Feels impelled to act
Confidence	Prizes doubt	Maintains faith in practice
Source of justifications	Values theoretical explanations	Relies on empirical results, (e.g., "It works")
Search for knowledge	Reads research of others	Places value on personal experience
Uses of Knowledge	Prizes principles which account for differences between cases	Views each case as unique, stresses indeterminacy

Note. Concepts here based on Freidson's (1972) work.

Confidence

Practitioners tend to have confidence in the efficacy of their interventions. They are ready to persuade onlookers of the rightness of their practices even in the absence of robust evidence and, in fact, may feel threatened when others dare to challenge the claims made for what has been done in practice. Scientists, on the other hand, are inclined to doubt any claims; they call for data whenever conclusions seem too optimistic and sanguine. Scientists are disposed to ask "How do you know?" when it is alleged that an intervention is effective and lacking in long-range consequences. Doubt, almost cynicism, characterizes the mood of scientists in the face of a practical problem.

Source of Justification

Clinicians often claim that the efficacy of an intervention or a technique is justified because "it works" (Denemark & Nutter, 1984, p. 206). Scientists are generally suspicious of such a crude form of pragmatism. They are more interested in how the intervention worked, with the credibility of the claim that an intervention ought to work based on a particular model or paradigm that accounts for changes in the variables included within its scope. Whereas practitioners justify a proposed intervention on empirical grounds, scientists want to have a theoretical explanation of the empirical data to vouch for its legitimacy as a professional practice.

Search for Knowledge

Clinicians tend not to turn to scientific literature to acquire professional knowledge. Instead, much of their knowledge comes from personal, firsthand experiences. As Freidson (1972) stated:

> Indeed, the consulting professions in general and medicine in particular encourage the limitation of perspective by its members through ideological emphasis on the importance of firsthand, individual experience and on individual freedom to make choices and to act on the basis of such experience. Such emphasis is directly contrary to the emphasis of science on shared knowledge, collected and tested on the basis of methods meant to overcome the deficiencies of individual experience. (p. 347)

As suggested by Freidson's passage, scientists place more confidence in the professional literature, in the findings of research, and in the scholarly analyses of colleagues in the field.

Uses of Knowledge

Whereas scientists seek to discover laws or principles that have broad applicability to practice, clinicians are convinced that it is a fruitless search. They tend to view each case they face in practice as unique. Therefore, general rules or principles will not be of help to the practitioner. Whereas scientists generate production functions or describe treatment effects by charting differences between sample means, clinicians act on the belief that an intervention works with differential effects on individuals who receive it. They are less interested in the overall, mean effect, than in how a particular case (individual) responds to it.

Freidson did not claim that these aspects of mentality are independent, free-standing factors. Instead, they are mutually dependent and related. For example, the suspicion of law-like principles would discourage a clinician from relying on published research and would instead encourage him or her to place confidence in personal experiences. Similarly, the mutually reinforcing aspects of seeing something work weaken the disposition to inquire into the theoretical aspects of the intervention.

FUNCTIONALITY OF THE CLINICAL MENTALITY

Is it poor practice not to adopt a scientific rationality when practicing a profession, whether it be business, medicine, or teaching? Freidson (1972) answered this question in the negative by arguing that:

The [clinical] rationality is particularized and technical; it is a method of sorting the enormous mass of concrete detail confronting [the professional] in his individual cases. The difference between clinical rationality and scientific rationality is that clinical rationality is not a tool for the exploration or discovery of general principles, as is the scientific method, but only a tool for sorting the interconnections of perceived and hypothesized facts. (p. 171)

In short, being clinical is far from acting unprofessionally; quite the contrary, the dispositions that constitute this mentality are professionally highly valuable to individuals working in clinical settings.

At this point, our argument takes two turns from Freidson's work. First, we spend the rest of this chapter discussing teaching and not medicine, although it was a study of the latter profession that informed Freidson's work on clinical mentality. Clearly, the professions of medicine and education are quite different. Although wary of using the comparison as a basis of proof or as critical assumptions in our argument, we do think the two professions are similar in significant ways. Both professions deal with individuals in a setting that presses for action and that is, by and large, complex and to some extent indeterminate. Further, some evidence suggests that teachers adopt a mentality very similar to that attributed to the clinicians in Freidson's study (Doyle & Ponder, 1977–78, pp. 1–12).

The second turn is from teaching to teacher education. Eventually, we discuss the mentalities of teacher educators. We are convinced that mentalities are determined in large measure by the press of contexts in the world of work. Because most teacher educators are first teachers and only subsequently teacher educators, we describe how teaching and the demands of teaching shape the mentalities of teachers. If our argument is convincing, perhaps our claim, that teacher educators are more likely to possess clinical outlooks than their colleagues in the foundations of education where classroom experience is less likely a criterion of employment, will also be compelling.

If teacher educators are characterized as more clinical in their outlooks than their colleagues in the education professoriate, how did they get that way? Our judgment is that the task of teaching school, almost always a prerequisite for becoming a teacher educator, shapes the thinking habits of those engaged in the practice of public school teaching. In the following section, we describe characteristics of the contexts in which teachers, some of whom are to become teacher educators, practice their profession. These qualities, including the complexity of the task, the isolation of the classroom, and the state of the available research relevant to coping with the enduring problems of teaching, make clinical mentalities functional in the school setting.

Complexity of the Classroom

Only recently have researchers begun to understand the complexity of the teacher's life in the classroom. The emergent literature on the sociology of classrooms provides an explanation for the functionality of the clinical mentality for teachers who work under constraining organizational conditions and who must meet the pressing tasks of instruction and classroom management.

Far from the simple places classrooms were assumed to be until about 25 years ago, classrooms are now characterized as busy, crowded, and constraining. As Dreeben (1973) pointed out:

> Classrooms, where conscripted children are gathered in confined spaces over long spans of time, engender problems of compliance and order for teachers. From the teacher's perspective the central issue is engaging pupils in the instructional proceedings—keeping them interested, at work, and actively involved. The means for doing so, however, are not well understood so that one often finds teachers attempting to keep up with and control the rapid flow of events: in part the director of these events, in part their prisoner, but in any case deeply engrossed in them. . . . With the endemic uncertainty and unpredictability of classroom events, the teacher, in attempting to instruct and maintain order, becomes more the reactor to than the designer of classroom activities. (p. 463)

Many writers have discussed the isolation of the classroom teacher. One implication of the isolation is that the success or failure experienced by a teacher is often taken as a measure of that particular teacher's effort. That is, there is no one with whom to share responsibility when something fails. Any failures are not the school's failure or the district's failure, but the teacher's failure. In this setting, is there any wonder why teachers exhibit a disdain for being second guessed and why they cannot and do not entertain doubt about the efficacy of their interventions and methods? Expressions of doubt here can suggest they don't know what they are doing. And the persons who can least entertain doubt are those for whom uncertainty is most painful. How could teachers, thrust into situations such as this, not help but see the world in clinical terms, as described by Freidson (1972)?

Regardless of how a particular teacher balances all the imperatives of the job, the main point here is that, in one way or another, he or she must act. The job demands immediate actions and reactions, frequently in the face of uncertainty and unpredictability. Thus, the acid test of any action, under these pressing conditions is, "Does it work in this case?" That teachers often have to make decisions quickly in a complex environment suggests that intuition, acting on one's instincts, developing the ability to act on a gut level, would become highly functional. There is little time to pause, to reflect, to ponder, to be, in effect, scientific.

Lack of Reliable and Usable Research

As most practitioners know, there is no how-to-do-it manual for teachers that is the equivalent of the physician's *Merck Manual*. Standard procedures for coping with the enduring problems of teaching are notably absent. With no firm guidelines based in research or science to guide them, teachers find reflection, the consideration of alternatives, the search through books and research literature, or even the consultation with "experts" to be time-consuming and nonproductive. For example, how can teachers apply the research-supported causal generalization of the form, "Treatment X causes an increase in arithmetic achievement," when the data surely show that in the experiment that spawned the generalization, not all children gained, and some actually lost proficiency when, disregarding means, the patterns of individual student gains and losses are taken into account? To tell teachers to rely on mean scores is to disregard their outlook about the teaching task, in short, their mentality.

Without reliable evidence and under the compelling need to act, teachers must have the courage to try something out to see if it works. Freidson termed this approach "crude pragmatism" (p. 169). And because there are few guides, generalizations, or principles of scientific merit available to them, teachers tend to create personal principles. As Freidson (1972) recounted:

> "Principles" are generated in the course of clinical practice, but they are generalizations from clinical experience, which is to say, generalization from personal and systematically biased experience. As Oken has stated, "clinical experience" is frequently personal mythology based on one or two incidents, or on stories by colleagues. (pp. 171–172)

Tversky and Kahneman (1974) demonstrated how individuals, and presumably practitioners, when compelled to make judgments under uncertain conditions, rarely find analysis a functional approach. Instead, they work to simplify complex tasks by relying on a number of heuristic principles that are found to be useful (p. 1124).

CONSEQUENCES ACCRUING TO THOSE WITH CLINICAL MENTALITIES IN A UNIVERSITY SETTING

In the previous section, we suggested that clinical mentality is linked to the conditions under which teachers work. Turning now to higher education, we suggest that persons at the university who prepare others for clinical roles, such as teacher educators, are more likely to possess clinical mentalities than are their colleagues, who are less engaged in training functions.

Our assertion is based on several considerations. First, teacher educators are far more likely to have been recruited from the ranks of classroom teachers than are those who are engaged in research. The findings of Carter (1984) and Ducharme and Agne (1982) support the generalization that most teacher educators were at one time teachers in the schools. Although some may have left the school because in part they resisted adopting a clinical mentality and thus found teaching to be unmanageable or dissatisfying, those who came into clinical positions on a teacher education faculty may be likely to have clinical mentalities.

Second, although surely all professors are, as teachers, thrust regularly into a clinical role, for the researcher teaching does not represent a heavy emotional investment. Researchers are not often affected professionally by the quality of their classroom teaching. They are generally rewarded in terms of journal articles published or funds generated through proposal writing. Because the emotional commitment to teaching is comparatively weak, the press to become clinical when pondering the teaching act is less acute. Professors in these straits can distance themselves from the enduring problems of teaching. To a large degree, they can avoid issues of assessment, of being prepared, of being relevant. There is little call to take on clinical attitudes. On the contrary, to be successful in the scientific world of research, the attitudes and mentalities of the scientist are required.

Third, teacher educators are often primarily responsible for instruction in methods courses and supervision of field internships. In teaching methods courses, teacher educators focus more heavily on how-to aspects of various techniques than their theoretical bases. Because practice is the primary concern of methods courses, teacher educators tend to focus on such clinical issues as taking action and what works, and thus adopt the clinical point of view. Further, because teacher educators frequently are responsible for supervision of field experience, they are in closer contact with the public schools and with teachers than their colleagues and in fact must prepare candidates to function in the public school setting. The task then reinforces the mentality teacher educators are likely to have brought from their previous public school roles.

Thus, it seems that teacher educators are more likely to be clinically oriented, for many of the same reasons associated with the aforementioned work roles that apply to classroom teachers. The question is then: What happens to persons who manifest clinical mentalities in the university setting? Some tentative answers to this question follow.

Attitudes Toward Research

One attribute of the clinical mentality is an impatience with research reports and research findings, especially those of a statistical nature. The individual who works day in and day out with a variety of persons is not interested in reports of central tendency or estimates of variance explained. He or she needs to know what to do in particular cases, and there is precious little research that can tell him or her what to do. From this perspective, teacher educators often show their disdain for research and for the research process. They themselves do not engage in research; they find it uninformative. Further, they will share their negative views about research with their colleagues. They mimic the 10-minute rituals at the American Educational Research Association (AERA) meetings, and they laugh at the sophistication they consider "pseudo" found in the research reports published in the *American Educational Research Journal.* Their generalized lack of respect for research and their abstaining from doing any research redounds against them again and again. Prizing research is a norm of the Academy, and being derisive of such a norm engenders serious sanctions, both informal and formal.

Claims of Efficacy

One element of the clinical mentality is a powerful confidence in the efficacy of the interventions and other actions in which one is engaged. Because there are few standards of conduct and great difficulty exists in defending many of the decisions an instructor must make, those with clinical mentalities tend to make assessments of their own effectiveness based on what they see and how things work out, and most of them are positive. Researchers defend the quality of their work by counting the number of journal articles published or the number of dollars brought to the college or university through grant writing efforts. When the teacher educator presents data on his or her efficacy, he or she asks for his or her teaching to be recognized as of high quality and often is distraught when the act of teaching is seen as having little value unless its quality can be demonstrated. Of course, the quality is demonstrated to the instructor by what he or she sees day in and day out. But there is some difficulty in communicating this quality to faculty committees allocating merit salary increases, so the teacher educator is often very low on the merit list. The evidence that seems relevant in making salary merit decisions to those with clinical mentalities is rejected by those who think scientifically.

Difficulty in Exchanging Views

We have characterized the two mentalities found in university settings as tantamount to two cultures. Nowhere is that analogy more apt than in efforts for members of these two sects to communicate with one another. It is similar to persons from different cultures trying to share their views. Each fails to speak the language of the other, and instead of responding to apparent dissonance with wonderment or with additional effort to listen more carefully or speak with greater precision, the participants tend to become angry and disrespectful.

In sum, the clinical mentality faculty are seen as norm-breakers. They place little value on research, they don't do research, and they don't apply research. And, as is often the case in any organization or society, those who break the norms, or are perceived as norm-breakers, are sanctioned.

IMPLICATIONS

We have painted a picture that may appear quite grim. The tensions between these particular orientations surely affect teacher educators' feelings of satisfaction with their work, their sense of efficacy, and their reputations. And as Kimble (1984) remarked, the prospects for achieving harmony are not bright (p. 833). There are at least three implications to consider, if our descriptions are at all accurate.

First, if teacher education is to remain on the campus of major research universities, teacher educators must become bicultural. They will need to communicate in the cultures of both mentalities, respecting the norms and customs of both. Katz et al. (1982) carried out a study of the reputations of teacher educators and found that, by and large, the professors of a large midwestern university saw teacher educators as being interested in the nitty-gritty of schools and too involved in practical matters to inquire into school problems with rigor. On the other hand, practicing teachers saw teacher educators as being sublimely involved in model building, theory testing, and writing research grants. Although both sets of reputations were different, both were pejorative. There is a need on the part of teacher educators to switch the reputations that this study suggested prevail. They must be seen as researchers and scholars by university faculty and as practitioners by the teachers in the community.

At present, there are some exceptional teacher educators who pass in both cultures. It would be desirable to do some case studies to find out how some individuals are able to succeed in both places, at the same time studying those who are able to excel in only one of the arenas. Perhaps a series of such studies could be instructive.

Second, we have made the point that the effectiveness of teacher educators is hindered by the divisiveness and stress they experience on university campuses due, in part, to cultural conflict. Clearly, one alternative is to assign teacher education functions to a special purpose institution removed from university settings. In such contexts, perhaps teacher educators would be better able to carry out their roles as trainers of teachers. In short, this recommendation is a call for a return to the normal school. Normal schools enjoyed a clear mission, and the resources assigned to teacher education were utilized on its behalf. Now, teacher education does not receive its share of the university budget, and the more glamorous research efforts are the ones that receive high priority, not perhaps on graduation day when the parents of undergraduates are in the audience, but on the occasion when the budgets are framed and pay raises are determined (Peseau & Orr, 1980). Perhaps separation is an option that needs further study, especially given the analysis we have presented in this chapter.

A third, more modest, implication should be considered. If it is impractical to reopen normal schools, perhaps teacher educators and teacher education programs should be isolated in the university—with their own school and their own budgets. Functioning like law schools or medical schools, schools of teacher education could stop fencing with senate committees or with the politics of academic affairs found within the college structure. (This suggestion does not assume that law schools or medical schools are not engaged in campus politics, but they don't have to negotiate hard to change curricula or to reward professors who make significant contributions in arenas not recognized by a vice-chancellor for academic affairs.) Organized instead under administrators committed to the education of teachers, colleges and schools of teacher education would be in a better position to chart their own destinies without worrying about the annual sanctions delivered to them by their colleagues in the college who are disdainful of training as a function and who prize only the production of scholarly work.

REFERENCES

Carter, H. (1984). Teachers of teachers. In L.G. Katz & J.D. Raths (Eds.), *Advances in teacher education* (Vol. 1, pp. 125–143). Norwood, NJ: Ablex.

Dearden, R.F. (1983). *Theory and practice in education.* London: Routledge & Kegan.

Denemark, G.W., & Nutter, N. (1984). The case for extended programs of initial teacher preparation. In L.G. Katz & J.D. Raths (Eds.), *Advances in teacher education* (Vol. 1, pp. 203–246). Norwood, NJ: Ablex.

Doyle, W., & Ponder, G.A. (1977–78). The practicality ethic in teacher decision making. *Interchange, 8*(3), 1–12.

Dreeben, R. (1973). The school as workplace. In R.M.W. Travers (Ed.), *Second handbook of research on teaching* (pp. 450–473). Chicago: Rand McNally.

Ducharme, E.R., & Agne, R.U. (1982). Education professoriate: A research based perspective. *Journal of Teacher Education, 33*(6), 30–36.

Freidson, E. (1972). *Profession of medicine.* New York: Dodd, Mead & Company.

Katz, L.G., Raths, J.D., Irving, J., Kurachi, A., Mohanty, C., & Sani, M. (1982). *Reputations of teacher educators among members of their role set.* Paper presented at the annual meeting of the American Educational Research Association, New York City.

Kimble, G.A. (1984). Psychology's two cultures. *American Psychologist, 39*(8), 833–839.

Peseau, B.A., & Orr, P.G. (1980). The outrageous underfunding of teacher education. *Phi Delta Kappan, 62*(2), 100–102.

Schwab, J.J. (1978). The practical: A language for curriculum. In I. Westbury & N.J. Wilkof (Eds.), *Science, curriculum and liberal education: Selected essays* (pp. 287–321). Chicago: University of Chicago Press.

Sergiovanni, T.J. (1985). Landscapes, mindscapes, and reflective practice in supervision. *Journal of Curriculum and Supervision, 1*(1), 5–17.

Snow, C.P. (1959). *The two cultures and the scientific revolution.* London: Cambridge University Press.

Tversky, A., & Kahneman, D. (1974, September). Judgment under uncertainty: Heuristics and biases. *Science, 185,* 1124–1131.

Chapter 4

Teacher Planning, Collegiality, and the Education of Teachers: A Developmental Integration of Research-Validated Knowledge with Practice*

Peter P. Grimmett

Director, Centre for the Study of Teacher Education
University of British Columbia

The last decade or so has produced a burgeoning number of studies of teaching and teacher education, such that Berliner (1987) maintained that we have the beginnings of a body of knowledge. This body of knowledge would seem to hold implications for the education of teachers.

Research on teaching has produced findings on several important topics of general pedagogy, such as teacher planning and decision making, classroom management, active/explicit teaching, teacher expectations and student motivation, and cooperative learning. Each of these topics could be regarded as constituting an essential component

---

* I wish to acknowledge the help and support extended by my colleagues Pat Crehan, Gaalen Erickson, Ted Riecken, and Alan MacKinnon in the work undertaken in this chapter. I also wish to give inordinate praise to Cindy Drossos whose word processing skills have completely dissipated my fear of deadlines.

of a teacher education program (see Berliner, 1987). Research in teacher education has produced studies of those who teach teachers, studies of students of teacher education, studies of the curriculum of teacher education, and studies about the milieu of teacher education (see Lanier & Little, 1986).

Purpose of the Chapter

The purpose of this chapter is three-fold:

1. to report research on teacher planning (as an example of research on teaching) and research on teacher collegiality (as an example of research in teacher education) and derive implications for the teacher preparation process;
2. to develop a framework for understanding how research findings can be integrated developmentally with practice in teacher education; and
3. to illustrate, through application of the framework to research on teacher planning and teacher collegiality, how research-validated knowledge can be used to further the development of preservice teachers.

Focus of the Chapter

This chapter focuses on how findings from research on teaching (illustrated by teacher planning research) and research in teacher education (illustrated by research on teacher collegiality) can be integrated developmentally into the education of teachers. The chapter has three sections. The first one gives an overview of research on teacher planning in terms of the different findings for prospective and experienced teachers and derives from the findings implications for the teacher preparation process. The second section reports research on teacher collegiality in terms of the different findings for prospective and experienced teachers and also attempts to derive implications for practice at the preservice level. The third section attempts to bring the findings from the two bodies of research together in the form of a developmental integration. A framework is proposed to highlight a parallel and complementary form of development to the prospective-experienced teacher continuum emerging in the research findings. This other form of development takes place along a continuum framed by the differential expectations associated with the various ways in which teachers use research-validated knowledge. This framework is then applied to selected aspects of the research findings reported to show how the knowledge generated about teacher planning can be used within an environment grounded in collegiality.

TEACHER PLANNING AND IMPLICATIONS FOR TEACHER PREPARATION

Research on teacher planning is presented to illustrate how implications from any area of research on teaching can be derived for the teacher preparation process. Teacher planning is chosen not because it is more important than the others but because it is one area of teaching that likely addresses some of the initial concerns of student teachers. It represents a starting point and a foundation without which it is difficult to understand and practice something as innovative and complex as active/explicit teaching and/or cooperative learning. What, then, does research on teaching in the area of teacher planning have to say that is of relevance to teacher preparation?

Most research on teacher planning is based on a conception of teaching as a decision-making process. Shavelson and Stern (1981) suggested that this conception rests on two assumptions: first, that teachers are practitioners who, like other professionals such as physicians, make reasonable judgments (i.e., they operate rationally within the limits of their information processing capabilities) and carry out decisions in an uncertain, complex environment; and second, that teachers' behaviors are guided by their thoughts, judgments, and decisions. Research on teacher planning is therefore one component of research on teacher thinking, the most recent reviews of which are to be found in Clark and Peterson (1986) and Clark and Yinger (1987). This program of research has produced descriptions of the purpose and types of planning and of which factors teachers take into account as they plan and select instructional activities.

The Purpose and Types of Planning

Teacher planning can be thought of as selecting appropriate ways of delivering instruction. Clark and Yinger (1987) report that teachers generally have a three-fold purpose when planning for instruction. Teachers plan: a) to meet immediate personal needs, for example, to reduce the uncertainty presented by the classroom and their own resulting anxiety, to find a sense of direction, confidence, and security; b) as a means to the end of instruction; that is, teaching the material, collecting and organizing materials, organizing time and activity flow; and c) to have direct use of the plan during instruction; that is, to organize pupils, to get an activity started, to act as an aide memoire, and to provide a framework for instruction and evaluation. In carrying out this three-fold purpose, Clark and Yinger (1979) found that teachers generally make, at different times, eight types of plans, namely, yearly, term, unit, weekly, daily, lesson, long-range, and short-range plans. Of these, unit plans were identified by teachers as being the most important type of plan, followed by weekly and daily plans. Only 7% of the 78 teachers sampled in the Clark and Yinger (1979) study regarded lesson plans as serving an important function.

This is in sharp contrast to the finding of Griffin et al. (1983) that student teachers are preoccupied not with unit, weekly, or daily plans but with planning lessons. They further found that this tendency was reinforced explicitly and implicitly by cooperating teachers, university supervisors, and the protocols of teacher education programs. Not surprisingly, they found student teachers to be relatively unconcerned and uninformed about how to plan sequences of instruction for a period as long as a school year or as short as a 2- or 3-week unit. Griffin (1983) took issue with the contrast found between the planning practices of experienced teachers and student teachers. He suggested that prospective teachers be given opportunities to plan curricula and practice long-range planning but not in a manner that is distanced, temporally and ideologically, from the classroom.

A different view on preservice preparation was proposed by Borko and Niles (1987). They described how, when asked what they might want to know to improve their planning, experienced teachers essentially responded "nothing—we are doing just fine with this important teaching activity" (p. 179). They went on to speculate that experience may be a major determining factor in teachers' concerns about planning. Experienced teachers appear to reach a point at which their planning fulfills their needs for organization, acceptable activity flow, and psychological comfort. Borko and Niles characterized this as a "planning plateau" (p. 180). They then accounted developmentally for preservice and beginning teachers. Using Feiman-Nemser's (1983) conceptualization of learning to teach, Borko and Niles (1987) posited that, because preservice teachers have instructional needs and priorities that are dissimilar to those of experienced teachers, the literature on planning may prove to be differentially useful to teachers, depending on where they are developmentally. They cited responses in their own research to two questions: "How have you changed as a planner since you began teaching?" and "What are the three most important things you tell your student teachers about planning?" (p. 180). The responses seemed to reflect changing needs and priorities in teachers' minds as they developed from prospective to experienced teacher. The experienced teachers in the sample reported that their suggestions for student teachers revolved around lesson plans rather than unit, weekly, or other forms of long-range plans. Yet when they talked about their own planning, these experienced teachers reported that they were now able to plan for individual pupils and groups more effectively, that they knew the subject-matter content better, and that they were better equipped to teach to long-range plans.

Thus, if the teachers' self-report data in Borko and Niles' (1987) study are accurate representations of reality, it is possible to conclude from their discussion that the emphasis at the preservice level on lesson plans, which Griffin (1983) called into question, may be developmentally appropriate. That is not to suggest that lesson plans should be the sole focus in preparation programs; rather, a sound grasp of how to plan a lesson appears to be foundational to learning how to make other types of long-range plans. Further, the process of learning to teach helps prospective teachers recognize the role that long-range plans play in the facilitation of classroom instruction. The initial emphasis in teacher education programs would seem, then, to be more appropriately focused on the formulation of lesson plans, but accompanied by an advance organizer of some of the other types of plans whose utility student teachers will grow to appreciate the more they become immersed in the practice of teaching.

Factors Taken into Account in Planning Instruction

The model of teacher planning proposed by Tyler (1950) (i.e., beginning with the formulation of objectives, the selection and organization of content, the selection and organization of activities, and ending with the evaluation of learning outcomes) has not been found in studies of teacher planning (Taylor, 1970; Zahorik, 1975) to be consistent with actual practice. Rather, teachers tend to plan focusing primarily on content and activities, disregarding both the linear sequence and the emphasis on objectives that Tyler proposed. The factors that teachers take into account in planning instruction generally revolve around how they select content and activities for student learning. The major (and, in some cases, only) influence on teachers' selection of content would appear to be the textbook. Subject-matter concerns in planning quickly become concerns about how to present textbook-prescribed content. Consequently, the selection of activities comprises the principal focus of teachers' instructional planning. Doyle and Carter's (1987) synthesis of how teachers choose the means of instruction suggested that four broad factors influence this selection process: pupil engagement; room arrangement; complexity of an activity; and time allocation.

Pupil engagement.   Teachers choose activities according to how they think a particular task or activity will promote high levels of pupil involvement.

Room arrangement. Because the classroom presents a complex environment for instruction, teachers take time to set up the physical arrangement of the classroom carefully. Teachers seem to know that "the way desks are turned, the distance between desks, the location of supplies, and the patterns for traffic in the room have important consequences for classroom order" (Doyle & Carter, 1987, p. 192).

Complexity of an activity. The general principle here is that the more complex the activity, the more teacher energy is required to establish and sustain it.

Time allocation. Doyle and Carter (1987, p. 193) maintained that one of the critical tasks a teacher faces in classrooms is that of scheduling activities to fit the time available. Teachers at all levels have to plan for the initiation, duration, and closure of activities within content areas and specifically need backup work activities to keep early-finishing students productively engaged in the learning process.

Griffin et al. (1983) produced findings that demonstrate how different student teachers are from experienced teachers when it comes to choosing instructional activities. The teacher candidates studied by Griffin and colleagues received minimal (if any) assistance in determining which data sources were available for or appropriate to making instructional decisions. Moreover, student teachers had almost no opportunities to group or regroup pupils for instruction and consequently experienced little or no practice in diagnosis and prescription to match learner needs with instructional activities. Griffin (1983) argued that information about how to select instructional activities appropriately should be made available to prospective teachers along with opportunities to practice the matching of learner needs with instructional activities. But this is tantamount to framing as expectations for prospective teachers those behaviors that have been found to be present in experienced teachers. Such a view overlooks that student teachers are learning to teach. It would seem more plausible to argue that the efficient selection of appropriate learning activities constitutes a goal of teacher education rather than the means whereby novices are prepared. Prospective teachers need to be grounded in how to select instructional content and activities according to the objectives set for a given lesson. They can also be exposed to the fact that experienced teachers typically plan by focusing on content and activities with little or no regard for objectives or evaluation. But, as Borko and Niles (1987) pointed out, they also need to understand why the planning practices of experienced teachers have evolved in this way. Experienced teachers have, over time, become adept at abstracting learning intents out of curriculum materials and instructional activities such that they do not, at this point in their development, perceive a need to write out objectives. It does not follow, then, that student teachers can be expected to acquire during preparation what has taken experienced teachers years of practice to accomplish. An emphasis on the formulation and derivation of objectives at the preservice level may be an essential precursor to developing the sophistication in planning and selecting learning activities that comes through the rigorous experience of practice. Such an emphasis would not preclude but would lead into the selection of activities according to appropriate data sources with opportunities for student teachers to match learner needs with instructional activities. The important point is that prospective teachers should not attempt to do what experienced teachers typically do without first exploring, understanding, and internalizing the notion of intentionality, which is central to any form of instructional planning.

Doyle and Carter's (1987) point that teachers need backup work activities to keep early-finishing students productively engaged in the learning process suggests a further implication for prospective teachers learning to plan for instruction. Student teachers need to engage in what Borko and Niles (1987, p. 181) referred to as "overplanning." That is, they should be encouraged to plan more than enough activities for a given time period, but not in the form of detailed scripts that could hinder the lesson flow and create the kind of rigidity that Zahorik (1970) found present in teachers whose plans contained considerable specificity of detail. Rather, to use Doyle's (1984) metaphor of viewing the curriculum as a lunar landscape, student teachers should learn to plan more and more gaps for pupils to encounter and cross by operations that they (the pupils) perform for themselves.

Summary

Figure 1 summarizes the findings from research on teacher planning for prospective and experienced teachers. Prospective teachers generally differed from experienced teachers in terms of the types of plans used and the factors taken into account in making such plans. Although all teachers used plans for similar purposes (i.e., to reduce uncertainty, to act as an instructional means, and as an aide memoire), prospective teachers tended to focus on short-range lesson plans for total group instruction, whereas experienced teachers emphasized long-range unit plans that accommodated the learning needs of individuals and groups. The selection of content and activities in prospective teachers' short-range lesson plans tended to follow the Tylerian model in that all content and activities were selected according to the objectives of the

Planning Research	Prospective Teachers	Experienced Teachers
Types of Plans Used (1) to reduce uncertainty (2) as instructional means (3) as aide memoire	Short-range lesson plans for total group	Long-range units plans for individuals and groups
Factors taken into account in planning	*Focus on Tylerian model* Selection of content and activities according to lesson objectives	*Focus on selection of content and activities* Selection of content from textbook Selection of activities according to: pupil engagement room arrangement complexity of activity time allocation Objectives abstracted out of content and activities

FIGURE 1. Findings from teacher planning research for prospective and experienced teachers.

lesson. With experienced teachers this was not found to be the case. They did not select instructional activities according to lesson objectives but according to how complex any given activity was, how much time it required, how such an activity would promote pupil engagement, and how it would affect the existing physical arrangements in the classroom. Nor did experienced teachers select instructional content according to lesson objectives; rather, they allowed the content to be determined largely by the textbook and abstracted the lesson objectives out of the content and activities selected for the unit of work. Whereas prospective teachers emphasized the planning of lessons for total group instruction and began with the formulation of objectives that they used to anchor the selection of instructional content and activities, experienced teachers focused on the planning of units of work for individuals and groups, a process in which they selected content and activities according to the textbook and certain classroom-related factors and subsequently derived lesson objectives from the content and activities selected.

The knowledge base for teaching is not, however, limited to findings coming out of research on teaching. Shulman (1987) characterized the knowledge base as having the following categories:

- content knowledge;
- general pedagogical knowledge, with special reference to those broad principles and strategies of classroom management and organization that appear to transcend subject matter;
- curriculum knowledge, with particular grasp of the materials and programs that serve as "tools of the trade" for teachers;
- pedagogical content knowledge, that special amalgam of content and pedagogy that is uniquely the province of teachers, their own special form of professional understanding;
- knowledge of learners and their characteristics;
- knowledge of educational contexts, ranging from the workings of the group or classroom, the governance and financing of school districts, to the character of communities and cultures; and
- knowledge of educational ends, purposes, and values, and their philosophical and historical grounds. (p. 8)

Of these categories, findings from research on teaching (illustrated here by teacher planning research) fall into those of general pedagogical knowledge and, to a lesser extent, knowledge of educational contexts. Findings from research in teacher education (illustrated here by teacher collegiality research), on the other hand, would appear to fall more into the categories of pedagogical content knowledge and knowledge of educational contexts than the category of general pedagogical knowledge.

COLLEGIALITY AND IMPLICATIONS FOR PREPARATION PROGRAMS

This section reports the findings of those studies that describe how teachers were socialized to the norms of collegiality and experimentation (Little, 1981, 1982) and derives implications thereof for the preparation of teachers. The rationale for this focus is that many beginning teachers lack the support that collegiality affords, and most teacher preparation programs do little to break student teachers from the predominant norms of self-sufficiency, privacy, reticence (Chism, 1985), immediacy, and individualism (Jackson, 1968; Lortie, 1975) that organizational conditions of cellular isolationism (Lortie, 1975) tend to promote. Many teachers have peers but no colleagues (Silver, 1973). This state of affairs is confirmed by studies that have documented the nature of collegial exchange in teaching (Bussis, Chittenden, & Amarel, 1976; Feiman-Nemser, 1983; Goodlad, 1984; Huberman, 1980; Lieberman & Miller, 1979) and found it to be fragmented and insubstantial. Goodlad (1984), for example, found that teachers function autonomously but that "this autonomy *seems* to be exercised in a context more of isolation than of rich professional dialogue about a plethora of challenging educational alternatives" (p. 186). For beginning teachers, mentoring relationships with experienced colleagues is the exception, not the rule (Little, 1981). And cooperating teachers appear reluctant to encourage student teachers to enter into the field experience practicum as colleagues (Griffin et al., 1983). Yet Little (1981, 1982, 1987) documented the benefits of collegiality to teaching as a profession, and Lortie (1975) argued persuasively that teaching will not become a profession until practitioners take collegial responsibility seriously.

What is Collegiality and How is it Established?
Little's (1981) study of the norms and work conditions conducive to school improvement highlighted four conditions that, when present, appear to cultivate norms of collegiality and experimentation in schools:

> Teachers engage in frequent, continuous and increasingly concrete and precise *talk* about teaching practice (as distinct from teacher characteristics and failings, the social lives of teachers . . .). By such talk, teachers build up a shared language adequate to the complexity of teaching, capable of distinguishing one practice and its virtue from another. . . .
> Teachers and administrators frequently *observe* each other teaching,

and provide each other with useful (if potentially frightening) evaluations of their teaching. Only such observation and feedback can provide shared *referents* for the shared language of teaching, and both demand and provide the precision and concreteness which makes the talk about teaching useful.

Teachers and administrators *plan, design, research, evaluate and prepare teaching materials together.* The most prescient observations remain academic ("just theory") without the machinery to act on them. By joint work on materials, teachers and administrators share the considerable burden of development required by long-term improvement . . . and make rising standards for their work attainable by them and by their students.

Teachers and administrators *teach each other* the practice of teaching. (pp. 12–13) (Author's emphasis)

In a follow-up study, Bird and Little (1983) found that schools in which these norms and conditions were present were afforded substantial latitude for developing and testing curriculum ideas. Teachers joined study groups to learn more about teaching, and this eventuated in agreements to try out selected practices in classrooms as a form of their own research as teachers. Teachers enjoying these conditions reported that collegial work added to the pool of available ideas and materials, the quality of solutions to curricular problems, and generally to their own confidence and competence as classroom teachers (Bird & Little, 1983; Grimmett, 1987). It was further found that norms of collegiality were established most effectively in schools in which the principal worked in collaboration with district supervisors to provide human and material resources to support teachers working together (Grimmett, 1987).

The Benefits of Collegiality
Dombart's (1985) practitioner's view from the inside is a powerful call for collegiality as a means of lifting teachers above their typical station of being mired in an unrewarding, denigrating workplace.

The paradox of education as a profession is that it attracts people with visions into a system designed to frustrate those visions . . . Love of subject and children impelled these people into the profession, and it is precisely what is driving them out of it or underground. . . . Experienced teachers do not talk about visions; it is too painful. Like soldiers at the front, we have learned to assume a flippant and hardened attitude. . . . So it is not that we are either shiftless or stupid that keeps us silent about visions. It is that we are tired—tired of being powerless pawns in a system that treats us either with indifference or disdain. . . . Take a look at the working world of the insider. You will find that it is not an atmosphere that nourishes visions. Though we teachers are numerous, we are virtually powerless. We affect none of the key elements in our working lives. (p. 71)

One consequence of this state of affairs is that many good teachers are opting to leave the profession (Rosenholtz, 1985, p. 350), causing researchers like Goodlad (1984) to suggest that "to get ahead in teaching is to leave it" (p. 188). Collegial work conditions are fostered, in part, to address this dilemma. They are designed to help teachers help one another in their quest to foster pupil achievement and development. To use Sizer's (1984) terminology, collegiality is a way of "empowering Horace" (p. 201), thereby releasing in teachers a dialogue around the rich knowledge they appear otherwise to withhold.

Little (1987) documented the benefits that teachers gain from close colleagues. Teachers derive instructional range, depth, and flexibility from working together. The structures of collaborative group work, for example, interclass visitation and observation and studying classroom-related issues together, enable teachers to attempt curricular-instructional innovations that they would probably not have tried as individuals. But it is not merely team work that produces this effect—it is the joint action that flows from the group's purposes and obligations as they shape the agreed task and its outcomes.

Teachers also derive influence among their ranks and respect from others, such as administrators, pupils, and parents, through collegial work conditions. "The more *public* an enterprise teaching becomes, the more it both requires and supports collective scrutiny" (Little, 1987, p. 496). This collective scrutiny breeds influence and respect among teachers. The highest levels of reciprocal influence reported by teachers in studies conducted by Meyer, Cohen, Brunetti, Molnar, and Lueders-Salmon (1971) at Stanford were reserved for schools in which teachers were both routinely visible to one another and routinely and intensively involved in teams. It would appear, then, that a combination of visibility (planning for teaching and actual classroom instruction is carried out in the presence of other teachers), shared responsibility, and widespread interaction heightens the influence of teachers on one another and on the school as a whole.

Little (1987) also suggested that teachers derive career rewards and daily satisfaction from conditions of collegiality. Working with colleagues helps teachers to shape their perspectives on their daily work. It also enables them to reduce what Lortie (1975) referred to as "the endemic uncertainties of teaching" (p. 134), which typically deny teachers a sense of success. Little (1987) described this specific benefit in the following way:

> Instead of grasping for the single dramatic event or the special achieve-
> ments of a few children as the main source of pride, teachers [enjoying
> conditions of collegiality] are more able to detect and celebrate a pattern
> of accomplishments within and across classrooms. (p. 497)

Professional recognition, professional involvement, and professional
influence become rewards that keep teachers career-oriented and help
them establish a high sense of efficacy.

The research on collegial conditions in the workplace would seem
to hold important implications for the induction of beginning teachers
into the work force and for the preparation of prospective teachers.

Collegiality and Teacher Induction

Many studies have found that the teacher induction process is abrupt
and unstaged (Lortie, 1975; Feiman-Nemser, 1983) and a sink or swim,
"trial-by-fire" experience (Ryan, 1970; Little, 1981). Copeland and Jamgochian (1985) argued that this state of affairs serves neither teachers
nor students well. In its place, they proposed mechanisms for mutual
assistance and support. In a similar vein, Clark (1984) suggested that
a beginning teacher is more appropriately viewed as a well-started
novice to whom the subtleties and complexities of effective teaching
should be gradually introduced.

The kind of support and assistance referred to here is, to use Little's
(1987) distinction, thoroughly professional as well as social. It seeks to
do more than put new teachers at ease (as is generally the case in
schools); its primary purpose is to provide the kind of professional
support that advances beginning teachers' understanding and practice
of classroom instruction. Veenman (1984) pointed out that beginning
teachers' success or failure in classrooms cannot be traced to the presence
or absence of social support and general friendliness of the established
teaching staff; rather, these well-started novices are influenced by professional encounters that help to establish their confidence and competence
as classroom teachers. Little (1987, pp. 498–501) laid out the case for
mentoring and "learning to teach" school environments as powerful
mechanisms for assisting beginning teachers in their induction into the
work force.

Collegiality and Teacher Preparation

What research has found in the area of teacher induction also pertains
to the preservice level of preparation. Preservice teachers are novices
who appear to need considerable professional support if they are to
establish patterns of pedagogical thought and behavior that orient them
to new learnings and discoveries about teaching. Yet Griffin et al. (1983)

found that encounters between student teachers and their assigned university and school-based supervisors were typically infrequent, unfocused, and uncoordinated. Further, when student teachers were placed in collegial schools (similar in environment to those described in Little's 1981 landmark study), Lipsitz (1983) found that these environments were not automatically hospitable and supportive to student teachers. Schools that have the organizational conditions and work norms capable of fostering the continued development of experienced, pedagogically sophisticated teachers may not always be oriented to helping novices learn to teach. The standard of productivity, fast pace, shared language and understanding, and accumulated knowledge base of established colleagues working together could provide undue pressure for student teachers and thereby hinder rather than facilitate their development. Because it may provide too much too quickly for most student teachers, Little (1987) argued that this kind of demanding learning situation may best be reserved for experienced teachers. Koehler (1988) contested Little's interpretation, suggesting that teachers in collegial schools provide a better environment for student teachers than those in typical schools, and that collegial schools must reorganize to adjust to the level of development in most student teachers. Alternatives need to be found, therefore, that promote experiences of collegiality at the preservice level similar in intensity and professional support to those found by Little (1981) at the inservice level.

One alternative proposed here is to frame the program in such a way as to expose prospective teachers to the perspectives and habits that constitute collegiality. Copeland and Jamgochian (1985) and Gunstone and Northfield (1988) documented how this can be achieved by organizing students into support groups or teams in which each is made responsible for the learning of others. Because the transition from learner to teacher is fundamental and difficult, prospective teachers need a learning-to-teach environment that is conducive to growth. Such an environment would be analogous to, but different from, the collegiality evidenced among experienced teachers. The pitch of such an environment would be at the developmental level of novices. The purpose of learning to teach in collegial teams would be to provide support for students as they begin their professional socialization. Professional socialization for prospective teachers can be conceived of as a journey from a state of dependence through independence to collegial interdependence. Such a process would presuppose an orientation toward a conception of teacher autonomy (so essential to competent classroom practice) derived through positive interdependence rather than mutual isolation. Such a conception of teacher autonomy would carry with it a notion of professional responsibility; such a socialization process could disarm accountability of its unfortunate, pejorative connotations.

Yet, if students are to be viewed as novice teachers, they do not, by definition, know much about teaching nor perform its practice competently. Collegiality in itself may not, at this level, be sufficient to socialize prospective teachers to the desired ends of competent performance and professional responsibility. That is where mentoring fits in. Collegial teams of 15 or so students could, for the purposes of the school experience, be split into groups of five, each of which would be mentored by one faculty advisor and two cooperating teachers. Because of the smallness of scale used, all five students in a group could be placed in the same school; further, because fewer university and school personnel would be required overall to run the school experience component, the selection process could rigorously follow carefully thought-out criteria. Five primary criteria for mentors come to mind: (a) that they are knowledgeable about and skillful at teaching, (b) that they can demonstrate such knowledge and skills proficiently in classroom practice, (c) that they can reflect on their own teaching, (d) that they can engage others in reflection on teaching, and (e) that they have the disposition to work collegially with others as respected professionals.

Placing the group within one school with only two cooperating teachers implies that students can never assume a 100% load. But the idea that they, as novices learning to teach, should do so is unrealistic. The purpose of the practicum, it can be argued, is not to test whether students can "hack" the pressures of daily teaching. That would be like asking a medical student to take on the pressures of being a full partner in a general practice and still complete important studies and exams. Rather, the purpose, as Feiman-Nemser (1983) pointed out, is to provide an environment in which students can learn to teach. Consequently, the arrangement being proposed is designed to foster more important virtues and dispositions than the hard-tempered tenacity and stamina required to complete a difficult obstacle course. The dispositions to be nurtured are those that orient students toward collegial learning and reflection as a basis for the continued development of teaching as a profession once they have entered the work force. Prospective teachers placed in a small group in one school with two cooperating teachers and one faculty advisor would be expected to practice collegiality; that is, they would talk to one another about teaching, they would engage in shared planning and preparation, they would observe one another teach and engage in group reflective analysis after observation, and they would learn together and teach one another carefully selected instructional practices. The practice of collegiality would initially be demonstrated by the advisor and cooperating teachers, who would gradually induct the students into the process. In this manner, the student teaching experience foreshadows the kind of professionalism and sense of efficacy in teachers that researchers like Little (1981) and Ashton, Webb, and Doda (1982) found to be vibrant aspects of effective schools without, it is hoped, the disadvantages that Lipsitz (1983) found to accompany such experiences in so-called collegial schools.

Summary

Figure 2 summarizes the findings from research on teacher collegiality for prospective and experienced teachers. Prospective teachers generally differed from experienced teachers in terms of their typical practices and the benefits they were found to derive from collegiality. Silver's (1973) distinction between teachers with peers and teachers with colleagues has been used as an organizing frame for the findings pertaining to both prospective and experienced teachers. The findings about the typical practices of prospective teachers were found to be infrequent, unfocused, and uncoordinated. Further, prospective teachers were generally not encouraged by cooperating teachers to enter into the practicum experience as a colleague. Rather, left to their own devices in a trial-by-fire, sink-or-swim experience, they were found to socialize themselves to norms of individualism, isolationism, and self-sufficiency. The findings about the typical practices of prospective teachers are but a fore-shadowing of what was found to be typical for experienced teachers who only had peers and no colleagues. Experienced teachers with peers were found to adhere to similar norms and, in so doing, provided a stark contrast to experienced teachers with colleagues. Experienced teachers with colleagues were found to engage in practices of visibility, shared responsibility, and widespread interaction wherein they talked about teaching, observed one another teaching, planned together, and taught one another different instructional practices.

The findings about the benefits of collegiality also produced discrepancies between prospective and experienced teachers and between teachers with peers and teachers with colleagues. Prospective teachers tended to be so preoccupied with survival concerns that they did not attempt to consider the various instructional options available to them. In the one study reported in which prospective teachers were placed in a collegial school environment, it was found that this experience provided too much too soon for teachers at this level of development. For experienced teachers, the findings about the benefits of collegiality mirrored those about typical practices. Experienced teachers with peers were found to be given to frustrated visions, to perceiving themselves

Collegiality Research	Prospective Teachers		Experienced Teachers	
	Peers	*Colleagues*	*Peers*	*Colleagues*
Typical Practices	Not encouraged to enter into collegial experience Socialized to norms of individualism, isolationism, and self-sufficiency Professional encounters infrequent, unfocused, and uncoordinated	Rare occurrences	Self-sufficient Isolated Individualistic Private Reticent	Visible Sharing responsibility Engaging in widespread interaction -talking about teaching -observing others teaching -planning together -teaching one another
Benefits of Collegiality	Preoccupation with survival concerns No consideration of options available	Collegial schools too much too soon for this level	Frustrated visions Teachers perceive themselves as powerless Common perception to get ahead is to leave teaching	Instructional range, depth, flexibility -study groups -pool of ideas/materials Influence and respect Confidence/competence improved Career rewards and satisfaction

FIGURE 2. Findings from collegiality research for prospective and experienced teachers.

as powerless pawns in the education game, and to believing the common perception that to get ahead is to leave teaching. By contrast, experienced teachers with colleagues were found to derive instructional range, depth, and flexibility through the use of study groups, the focus of which was on classroom-related instructional issues, and the pool of ideas and curricular-instructional materials that resulted from the sharing and deliberations of such study groups. They were also found to derive influence and respect among administrators, pupils, and other teachers from collegial work conditions. Further, experienced teachers with colleagues reported that their confidence and competence as classroom teachers had improved considerably, and this was found to lead to increased job satisfaction and the provision of certain intrinsic career rewards.

The section on teacher collegiality and teacher preparation ended with a proposal for an alternative approach to the practicum setting. The proposal called for study groups consisting of five teacher candidates, two cooperating teachers, and one faculty advisor to be set up in carefully selected school sites. These groups would experience mentored collegiality in a manner that enabled all participants to pursue rigorously important questions pertaining to the practice of learning to teach. The purpose of this proposal was to provide at the preservice level a form of support and mentoring analagous to what had been found at the inservice level in collegial schools. This proposed alternative would provide an environment within which to socialize prospective teachers away from the less desirable norms of self-sufficiency and individualism toward developmentally appropriate expressions of the more desirable norms of collegiality and experimentation.

Research on teaching (illustrated by teacher planning research in this chapter) has produced much knowledge that could constitute part of the content in a teacher education program. Research on teacher education (illustrated by teacher collegiality research here) has also produced much knowledge that could constitute part of the process of such a program. But how can one bring the two together in teacher education?

BRINGING CONTENT AND PROCESS TOGETHER IN TEACHER EDUCATION: A DEVELOPMENTAL INTEGRATION

This section attempts to grapple with the question of how content and process can be brought together. At the outset, the assumption is made that the answer is complex, varying according to context, person, and situation. It is further assumed that to address the question adequately requires a careful conceptualization of how research-validated knowledge is understood and made use of by teachers as they reflect on their own practice.

A Framework for Understanding Teachers' Use of Research-Validated Knowledge

Kennedy (1984) argued that scientific knowledge is used in two different ways in making professional decisions: instrumentally and conceptually. Sergiovanni (1986) differentiated between these two ways of making decisions. He noted that instrumental decision-making views scientific knowledge as a body of artificial intelligence from which practitioners can draw standard treatments to apply to diagnosed problems, whereas conceptual decision-making seeks to establish augmented professional intelligence. This latter approach, Sergiovanni (1986) went on, views practitioners as being key aspects of the intelligence, and "augmented professional intelligence is intended to inform the intuitions of practitioners as they practice" (p. 354).

Fenstermacher (1980) also wrote about two ways to put research findings into practice: through rules and through discussion of evidence. Rules serve as a means for bridging educational research and practice when the results of research are converted into imperatives for teachers to follow. When using rules to communicate research findings, the recipient is directed to behave in ways that imitate the finding rather than being encouraged to consider the applicability of the research finding and the evidence on which it is based. Considering research findings through serious discussion of evidence was an alternative posed by Fenstermacher (1980) to communicating research findings by rules. In this manner, the evidence of research findings confronts the beliefs that teachers hold about their work while teachers, in turn, thoughtfully confront the meaning and applicability of findings researchers have generated. In weighing the evidence for research findings, teachers act as professionals who must carefully reject or adapt what research has found.

Whereas Kennedy (1984) and Sergiovanni (1986) wrote about ways of using research findings in making decisions, Fenstermacher (1980) addressed the question of how such findings could be justified when communicated to practitioners. Fenstermacher's rules and evidence not only seem to link with Kennedy's (1984) instrumental and conceptual decision-making processes respectively, but also presuppose different modes of thought. It would seem that communicating research-validated knowledge by rules presupposes Zumwalt's (1982) technological orientation; whereas communicating research-validated knowledge by discussion of evidence presupposes Zumwalt's deliberative orientation. Zumwalt (1982) characterized a technological orientation as seeing teaching "as being composed of a definable repertoire of knowledge, skills and attitudes that a teacher brings to bear in an effort to create certain changes in learners" (pp. 223, 224). The deliberative orientation, by contrast, regards teaching more as a clinical process of aggregating and making sense out of an incredible diversity of information sources that pertain to classroom teaching. This mode of thought emphasizes providing teachers with ways to think about their complex and contextually-influenced classroom experiences in light of research on teaching (Zumwalt, p. 237).

Zumwalt's two orientations would seem to have different associated expectations with respect to how research findings should relate to practice. The technological orientation, with its instrumental decision-making process relying on the communication of research-validated knowledge by rules, would seem to carry with it the associated expectation that teachers ensure that their practice conform to the rules and technologies that research findings have been used to validate. That is, research-validated knowledge is used to direct or control practice. The deliberative orientation, by contrast, with its emphasis on conceptual decision making and discussion of evidence, would seem to encourage teachers to choose among competing versions of good teaching according to the context, the situation, and anticipation of the consequences of following different lines of action for pupil learning. The associated expectation placed on teachers is that their deliberation on the evidence of research findings will inform practice.

So far, we have established two possible ways in which teachers can make use of research-validated knowledge: the instrumental approach, with its technological emphasis on research-derived rules to which practice is expected to conform, and the conceptual approach, with its deliberative orientation toward discussion of the evidence supporting research findings that are seen to inform practice. Figure 3 depicts these two approaches in terms of the basis of justification appealed to; that is, evidence or rules, the mode of thought/orientation operative, and the expectation for practice associated with each form of knowledge use.[1] But the figure also proposes a third possible way in which teachers could use research-validated knowledge. It is to a discussion of this that we now turn.

It is possible to argue that teachers derive the important concepts they use to structure their world and experiences not analytically, in the processing of information available to them (as Kennedy, 1984

---

[1] This figure is based on the thinking of Kennedy (1984), Sergiovanni (1986), Fenstermacher (1980), Zumwalt (1982), Lakoff and Johnson (1980), Connelly and Clandinin (1988), and Schön (1983, 1987, 1988), and should be regarded as suggestive of possibilities rather than exclusive or exhaustive.

Levels of Knowledge Use	Basis of Justification	Mode of Thought/Orientation	Associated Expectation for Practice
Metaphorical	Images	Reflective	Transform
Conceptual	Evidence	Deliberative	Inform
Instrumental	Rules	Technological	Conform

FIGURE 3. Three possible ways in which teachers make use of research-validated knowledge.

posited), but through experiential metaphors that permeate their thinking. Lakoff and Johnson (1980) introduced the notion of metaphor in
the following way:

> We have found . . . that metaphor is pervasive in everyday life, not just
> in language but in thought and action. Our ordinary conceptual system,
> in terms of which we both think and act, is fundamentally metaphorical
> in nature. The concepts that govern our thought are not just matters of
> the intellect. They also govern our everyday functioning, down to the
> most mundane details. Our concepts structure what we perceive, how we
> get around in the world, and how we relate to other people. Our conceptual
> system thus plays a central role in defining our everyday realities. If we
> are right in suggesting that our conceptual system is largely metaphorical,
> then the way we think, what we experience, and what we do everyday
> is very much a matter of metaphor. (p. 3)

Lakoff and Johnson (1980) essentially pointed to the way in which our
concepts are products of all our life experiences, personal biography,
and professional socialization. The metaphors that permeate our minds
structure how we think and act. For example, if one thinks of teachers
as responsible professionals, one would presume that there are reasons
for a teacher's classroom behavior that (even if the behavior per se
were dysfunctional) must first be explicated, respected, and considered
before that teacher can seriously be expected to undertake behavioral
changes. According to this metaphor, the imitation of new behaviors
that are inconsistent with the teacher's fundamental values and beliefs
about teaching is, at best, short-lived and, at worst, illusory.

Metaphors would seem to appeal to what Connelly and Clandinin
(1988) termed an *image*. Image, for Connelly and Clandinin, represents
a filament within teachers' experience, embodied in them as persons
and expressed and enacted in their practices and actions.

> An image reaches into the past, gathering up experiential threads mean-
> ingfully connected to the present. And it reaches intentionally into the
> future and creates new meaningfully connected threads as situations are
> experienced and new situations anticipated from the perspective of the
> image. Thus, images are part of our past, called forth by situations in
> which we act in the present, and are guides to our future. Images as they
> are embodied in us entail emotion, morality, and aesthetics. (Connelly
> & Clandinin, 1988, p. 60)

The identification of images seems to be associated with a reflective
orientation. Schön (1983, 1987, 1988) described how practitioners re-
flect-in-action as they attempt to create meaning of the problematic

aspects of a practice situation through problem setting and problem solving:

> In real world practice, problems do not present themselves to the practitioner as givens. They must be constructed from the materials or problematic situations that are puzzling, troubling and uncertain. . . . When we set the problem, we select what we will treat as the "things" of the situation, we set the boundaries of our attention to it, and we impose upon it a coherence which allows us to say what is wrong and in what directions the situation needs to be changed. Problem setting is a process in which, interactively, we *name* the things to which we will attend and *frame* the context in which we will attend to them. (Schön, 1983, p. 40) (Emphasis in original)

This reframing of a problem situation enables practitioners to make use of their existing "repertoire of examples, images, understandings, and actions" (Schön, 1987, p. 66). Reflection, thus, engages practitioners in a conversation with the problematic situation. Past experiences are brought to bear on the situation; frames are imposed that highlight certain aspects of phenomena at work in the situation; problems are set, the situation reframed, and problem-solving actions are generated. What practitioners essentially see in an uncertain situation of practice depends on what they make of the practice setting and the way in which they experimentally converse with the situation as they have framed it.

Problem setting and a reframing of the puzzling situation are central tenets to the view of reflection-in-action advanced by Schön (1983, 1987, 1988). The way we conceptualize a problem affects the solutions we develop. Schön also argued that we often think metaphorically as we frame problems and work toward their solution. Metaphorical thought combined with practical knowledge or images, to use Connelly and Clandinin's term, can lead us to tentative solutions to problem situations that are tested as the practitioner engages in a reflective conversation with the situation. In this way, reflection does not lend itself to the transfer of research-validated knowledge, but rather teachers who find that certain research findings have acted as a touchstone to their professional images can be characterized as using such knowledge metaphorically to transform practice.

Metaphorical transformation of practice would engage teachers in a seeing-as endeavour: That is, they see their classroom situations as researchers have seen the ones studied and attempt to act in their own situations as they understand the observed teachers would have done. In metaphorical transformation, research findings would function in teachers as a catalyst for seeing new puzzles in their classroom practice, enabling them to reframe tried-and-true patterns of classroom interaction in ways that permit exploration, experimentation, and subsequent improvement. In this manner, research-validated knowledge would not serve as arid theory devoid of practical implications but as a metaphor that facilitates the reconstruction of prevailing views and patterns of practice to lead to new understandings of teaching and classroom action. Such transformation of practice would, it seems, make for the kind of exciting intellectual inquiry that energizes classroom teachers for the stringent demands of teaching efficaciously.

The last sentence exposes the developmental bias built into Figure 3. Not only do teachers develop from prospective to experienced teachers, but they also develop from instrumental through conceptual to metaphorical ways of using research-validated knowledge. That is why the term "Levels of Knowledge Use" is used in Figure 3. These levels are seen as developmental stages; that is, higher stages reintegrate the structures of lower stages, and the goal of development is toward the higher stages. Progression from instrumental through conceptual to metaphorical levels of knowledge use should not, however, be equated with development from prospective to experienced teacher. Rather, the associated expectations of conforming, informing, or transforming one's practice[2] and development from one to the other could be operative in prospective and experienced teachers. What we have here are two parallel and complementary paths of development occurring at one and the same time. The parallels will become clear when the framework depicted in Figure 3 is applied to the research on teacher planning and teacher collegiality.

Applying the Framework to Teacher Planning and Teacher Collegiality Research

Figure 4 demonstrates how the different levels of knowledge use (represented by their associated expectations for practice, conform, inform, and transform) interrelate with the research on teacher planning and teacher collegiality (as summarized in Figures 1 and 2, respectively). Because of space, only one aspect of each (for planning—factors taken into account in planning instruction; for collegiality—typical practices) is presented to illustrate the interrelationship.[3]

---

[2] For a detailed explication of these expectations as they pertain to reflective practice, see Grimmett, MacKinnon, Erickson, and Riecken (1989).

[3] The interrelationships depicted in Figure 4 are strictly derivative, not empirical; that is, they represent hypothetical formulations based on and consistent with the imposition of a developmental continuum on the findings of research in the areas of teacher planning and teacher collegiality.

	Prospective Teachers	Experienced Teachers
Factors taken into account in planning instruction	C: Always begin lesson planning with the formulation of objectives and select content and activities accordingly.	C: Teachers should select lesson activities according to the factors of pupil engagement, room arrangement, complexity of activity, and time allocation.
	I: Factors open up other possible ways of planning lessons besides determining content and activities solely by objectives.	I: Factors unpacked by research serve as principles that guide deliberation about selection of lesson activities.
	T: Factors draw out experiences in teachers' repertoire/concerns about teaching and help to refigure basic conception of how to select content and activites appropriate to lessons in context.	T: Factors serve as metaphors enabling teachers to see the selection of lesson activities as the researchers do and in so doing reconstruct their understanding and practice of planning for classroom instruction.
Typical practices in collegiality	C: Teacher preparation should condition teachers to teamwork, insist on open-door teaching, break down nonprofessional norms.	C: Teachers should practice visibility, shared responsibility, and widespread interaction with one another around classroom teaching.
	I: Teacher preparation attempts to provide environment in which consideration of alternatives within and beyond survival level concerns and advice/feedback of colleagues is structurally reinforced.	I: Norms of collegiality provide one way of understanding the reform of work conditions and the structure of teaching.
	T: Stories of collegial practice elicit teachers' preconceptions about autonomy and professionalism, helping to transform them (or create anew) positive alternative conceptions of responsible practice.	T: Stories about collegial practices become part of teachers' personal, practical knowledge as they live in the daily rhythms and institutional constraints of the workplace.

C = Conform; I = Inform; T = Transform.

FIGURE 4. An example of how research findings about factors taken into account in planning instruction and about typical practices in collegialty can be interpreted according to instrumental, conceptual, and metaphorical ways of using research-validated knowledge.

The findings pertaining to factors taken into account in planning instruction would be interpreted differently by prospective and experienced teachers according to where they are developmentally on the Conform-Inform-Transform (CIT) continuum. Prospective and experienced teachers functioning instrumentally would tend to turn the findings into rules to govern practice. Prospective teachers at this level would seek to conform to the rule of always beginning lesson planning with the formulation of objectives and would attempt to select content and activities in accord with those objectives. Experienced teachers functioning at this level would attempt to conform to what research had found; that is, they would make a teacher-should statement of selecting lesson activities according to the factors of pupil engagement, room arrangement, complexity, and time allocation.

It is interesting to note that it is at the instrumental level of knowledge use that practitioners (and policy-makers) fall into the naturalistic fallacy of treating what is as grounds for what ought to be. Such a way of thinking is, by dint of what the processes involve, decidely absent from the conceptual and metaphorical levels of knowledge use.

Prospective teachers functioning at the conceptual level of knowledge use would look for ways in which the research findings could inform their practice. They would see the factors reported, such as pupil engagement, room arrangements, and so forth, as opening up other possible ways of planning lessons besides determining content and activities solely by objectives. Experienced teachers at this level of the CIT continuum would tend more to see the factors unpacked by research as serving as principles to guide deliberation about the selection of lesson activities.

The same research findings about factors taken into account in planning instruction would tend to be interpreted differently again by those prospective and experienced teachers who are at the level of metaphorical transformation of practice. Prospective teachers at this level would use the factors reported to draw out of their repertoire and/or concerns about teaching those experiences in the planning of instruction that have contributed to the construction of their basic conception of how to select content and activities in lessons. Once explicated, this conception could then be refigured or reconstructed in a manner wherein the factors would serve as symbolic representations of important considerations for planning lessons in context. For experienced teachers at this level, the transforming effect on practice would work out differently. For these teachers, the factors would serve as metaphors enabling them to begin to see the selection of lesson activities as researchers like Doyle and Carter (1987) did. They would attempt to grapple with how and why the teachers observed in the research selected their content and activities according to the four factors reported, and not others, and visualize their own selection process functioning analogously. This reconstructing of their understanding and experience of instructional planning would enlarge the teachers' basic conception of how to select activities and transform their practice of this professional task.

The findings about typical practices in collegiality also illustrate how prospective and experienced teachers at different levels on the CIT continuum interpret research-validated knowledge. Prospective teachers functioning instrumentally would likely expect the teacher preparation process to condition candidates to teamwork, to insist on open-door teaching, and to break down nonprofessional norms by directing candidates not to act in such ways. Experienced teachers would take a similarly conforming stance at the inservice level. They would expect teachers to be directed to practice visibility, to share professional responsibility, and to engage in widespread interaction with one another around classroom teaching. Anything less than a strongly-worded directive accompanied by suitable incentives they would interpret as not acting on the research.

For teachers at the conceptual and metaphorical levels of knowledge use, such an action would be an anathema. At the conceptual level teachers are seeking out information, whereas at the metaphorical level teachers want transforming stories of collegial practice.

Prospective teachers functioning at the conceptual level (inform) would tend to expect teacher preparation to provide an environment in which the consideration of alternatives within and beyond the survival level of concerns and the advice and critical feedback of colleagues (candidates and teacher educators) is structurally reinforced. Experienced teachers at this level would interpret the norms of collegiality as providing one way of understanding the current attempts, (e.g., Lieberman, 1988) to reform the work conditions and structure of teaching.

Teachers at the metaphorical level would likely use the research findings about typical practices in collegiality to stimulate the recovery and reconstruction of further stories of collegial practice. For "storytelling is the mode of description best suited to transformation in new situations of action" (Schön, 1988, p. 19). Stories are transforming because they are compelling and serve as a metaphor that facilitates the reconstruction of practice. For prospective teachers at this level, findings about typical practices in collegiality would act as stories, eliciting from candidates their preconceptions about autonomy and professionalism. These preconceptions could then be examined collectively in such a way as to help teacher candidates create anew positive alternative conceptions of responsible practice. For experienced teachers at this level, stories about collegial practices (those stimulated by the research findings and those coming through group sharing with colleague teachers) would tend to become an energizing component of their personal, practical knowledge as teachers live in the daily rhythms and institutional constraints of the workplace.

An Illustration of Developmental Integration

Return to the proposal for collegial study groups derived earlier in the chapter out of the research findings on typical practices in collegial schools. It should be clear from the preceding section that this proposal was not formulated as a way of directing practice but rather as a means whereby the practice of teacher candidates could be informed by the research findings and transformed by a supportive but challenging operationalization of the habits and perspectives that make up collegiality. But the proposal as it stands only represents a developmental integration of the different ways in which teacher candidates could make use of research-validated knowledge about collegiality. How does one add other research findings, for example, those from teacher planning, to the mix?

Integrating findings from teacher planning with those from teacher collegiality could put in jeopardy the collegial habits and perspectives the proposal is designed to cultivate. To countervail this possibility, one superimposes collegiality on the other research findings. In the case of our example, that would mean superimposing the findings about typical practices of collegiality on the findings about factors taken into account in instructional planning. In other words, in situations that present a forced choice, the process of collegial exchange is to be more highly valued than the acquisition of the content about planning. The purpose, then, is for teacher candidates to learn collegially what it means to select lesson content and activities appropriately. How, then, could they learn collegially about factors taken into account in planning in a manner that allows for development along the CIT continuum? The answer to this question will demonstrate the essence of what is meant here by a developmental integration of research-validated knowledge with practice.

The faculty advisor and the two cooperating teachers in each group could begin at the level of instrumental knowledge use (conform) with a focus on the notion of intentionality in planning and the role that objectives play in establishing and reinforcing the sense of direction that intentionality brings to a lesson. The reason for beginning at this level would be to expose teacher candidates to certain ground rules in planning with which their practice, at least initially, would be expected to conform. The teacher educators in each collegial group would have to read the candidates carefully to know when the latter were ready to receive information that might possibly create a sense of dissonance in some students. At an appropriate time, however, the teacher educators could introduce the findings about factors taken into account in instructional planning by experienced teachers as a means of informing the candidates' conception of intentionality and also stimulating collegial discussion of how the findings about factors could be or could not be integrated with the ground rules pertaining to the formulation of objectives. When the candidates are ready for a further transition, the teacher educators can move the group to the highest level of metaphorical transformation. Here they would develop and tell stories that would have embedded within them certain points about intentionality in the presentation of lessons and factors taken into account in selecting content and activities. For example, the story could be told of the chagrin experienced by two independent observers in a research project whose detailed field notes confirmed their nagging suspicion that the lessons they had observed were, in a word, pointless. That is, the teacher did not contextualize the lesson in terms of what had previously been learned, the objective was not stated (nor could the observers, who were adept at putting lessons together after-the-fact, find one, although the pupils seemed to understand what was happening and what they were expected to do), and closure occurred when the bell rang. As far as the observers could make out, the teacher had not a first clue about intentionality and its effect on lesson pacing, momentum, and direction. Or the story could be told of two contrasting teachers in the same school: one who taught with fluidity and poise, who had the children intrigued by the concepts introduced (and consequently had parents clamoring to have their children placed in that class), but who did not plan; and the other who taught extremely rigidly, prepared lessons meticulously, and insisted on covering all concepts, activities, and materials prepared even though at times the children appeared to have lost interest in the copious details that the teacher enjoyed. The purpose of these illustrative stories would be to stimulate thought and discussion around a possible theme of directionality with flexibility and the ultimate purpose and contribution of planning to the execution of teaching. The telling of stories would be used because they bring to life the research findings such that the practice of teacher candidates is not merely informed but, more importantly, transformed.

REFERENCES

Ashton, P., Webb, R., & Doda, N. (1982). *A study of teachers' sense of efficacy* (Final Report to the National Institute of Education #400-79-0075). Gainesville: University of Florida.

Berliner, D.C. (1987). Knowledge is power: A talk to teachers about a revolution in the teaching profession. In D.C. Berliner & B.V. Rosenshine (Eds.), *Talks to teachers: A Festschrift for N.L. Gage* (pp. 3–33). New York: Random House.

Bird, T.D., & Little, J.W. (1983). *Finding and founding peer coaching.* Paper presented at the annual meeting of the AERA, Montreal, Quebec.

Borko, H., & Niles, J.A. (1987). Descriptions of teacher planning: Ideas for teachers and researchers. In V.R. Koehler (Ed.), *Educators' handbook: A research perspective* (pp. 167–187). New York: Longman.

Bussis, A., Chittenden, E., & Amarel, M. (1976). *Beyond surface curriculum.* Boulder, CO: Westview Press.

Chism, N. (1985). *The place of peer interaction in teacher development: Findings from a case study.* Paper presented at the annual meeting of the AERA, Chicago, IL.

Clark, C.M. (1984). *Research on teaching and the content of teacher education.* Paper presented at the annual meeting of the AERA, New Orleans, LA.

Clark, C.M., & Peterson, P.L. (1986). Teachers' thought processes. In M.C. Wittrock (Ed.), *Handbook of research on teaching* (3rd ed., pp. 255–296). New York: MacMillan Publishing Company.

Clark, C.M., & Yinger, R.J. 91979). *Three studies of teacher planning.* (Research Series #55). East Lansing, MI: IRT, Michigan State University.

Clark, C.M., & Yinger, R.J. (1987). Teacher planning. In D.C. Berliner & B.V. Rosenshine (Eds.), *Talks to teachers: A Festschrift for N.L. Gage* (pp. 342–365). New York: Random House.

Connelly, F.M., & Clandinin, D.J. (1988). *Teachers as curriculum planners: Narratives of experience.* New York: Teachers College Press.

Copeland, W.D., & Jamgochian, R. (1985). Colleague training and peer review. *Journal of Teacher Education, 36*(2), 18–21.

Dombart, P.M. (1985). The "vision" of an insider: A practitioner's view. *Educational Leadership, 43*(3), 70–73.

Doyle, W. (1984). *Patterns of academic work in junior high school science, English, and mathematics classes.* Paper presented at the annual meeting of the AERA, New Orleans, LA.

Doyle, W., & Carter, K. (1987). Choosing the means of instruction. In V.R. Koehler (Ed.), *Educators' handbook: A research perspective* (pp. 188–206). New York: Longman.

Feiman-Nemser, S. (1983). Learning to teach. In L. Shulman & G. Sykes (Eds.), *Handbook of teaching and policy* (pp. 150–170). New York: Longman.

Fenstermacher, G.D. (1980). On learning to teach effectively from research on teaching effectiveness. In C. Denham & A. Lieberman (Eds.), *Time to learn.* Washington, DC: NIE.

Goodlad, J.I. (1984). *A place called school.* New York: McGraw-Hill.

Griffin, G.A. (1983). The dilemma of determining essential planning and decision-making skills for beginning educators. In D.C. Smith (Ed.), *Essential knowledge for beginning educators* (pp. 16–22). Washington, DC: AACTE.

Griffin, G.A., Hughes, R., Jr., Barnes, S., Defino, M., Edwards, S., Hukill, H., & O'Neal, S. (1983). *Clinical preservice teacher education: Final report of a descriptive study.* Austin, TX: R & D Center for Teacher Education, University of Texas.

Grimmett, P.P. (1987). The role of district supervisors in the implementation of peer coaching. *Journal of Curriculum and Supervision, 3*(1), 3–28.

Grimmett, P.P., MacKinnon, A.M., Erickson, G.L., & Riecken, T.J. (1989). Reflective practice in teacher education. In R. Houston, R. Clift, & M. Pugach (Eds.), *Encouraging reflective practice: An examination of issues and exemplars.* New York: Teachers College Press.

Gunstone, R.F., & Northfield, J. (1988). *A constructivist approach to teacher education.* Paper presented at the annual meeting of the AERA, New Orleans, LA.

Huberman, M. (1980). *Finding and using recipes for busy kitchens: A situational analysis of routine knowledge use in schools.* Washington, DC: NIE.

Jackson, P.W. (1968). *Life in classrooms.* New York: Holt, Rinehart & Winston.

Kennedy, M.M. (1984). How evidence alters understanding and decisions. *Educational Evaluation and Policy Analysis, 6,* 207–226.

Koehler, V.R. (1988). Barriers to the effective supervision of student teaching: A field study. *Journal of Teacher Education, 39*(2), 28–34.

Lakoff, G., & Johnson, M. (1980). *Metaphors we live by.* Chicago: University of Chicago Press.

Lanier, J.E., & Little, J.W. (1986). Research on teacher education. In M.C. Wittrock (Ed.), *Handbook of research on teaching* (3rd ed., pp. 527–569). New York: MacMillan Publishing Company.

Lieberman, A. (1988). *Building a professional culture in schools.* New York: Teachers College Press.

Lieberman, A., & Miller, L. (1979). The social realities of teaching. In A. Lieberman & L. Miller (Eds.), *Staff development* (pp. 54–68). New York: Teachers College Press.

Lipsitz, J. (1983). *Successful schools for young adolescents.* New Brunswick, NJ: Transaction Press.

Little, J.W. (1981). *The power of organizational setting: School norms and staff development.* Paper presented at the annual meeting of the AERA, Los Angeles, CA.

Little, J.W. (1982). Norms of collegiality and experimentation: Workplace conditions of school success. *American Educational Research Journal, 19*(3), 325–340.

Little, J.W. (1987). Teachers as colleagues. In V.R. Koehler (Ed.), *Educators' handbook: A research perspective* (pp. 491–518). New York: Longman.

Lortie, D.C. (1975). *Schoolteacher: A sociological study.* Chicago: University of Chicago Press.

Meyer, J., Cohen, E., Brunetti, F., Molnar, S., & Lueders-Salmon, E. (1971). *The impact of the open-space school upon teacher influence and autonomy: The effects of an organizational innovation* (Tech. Rep. #21). Stanford, CA: Center for Research and Development in Teaching, Stanford University.

Rosenholtz, S. (1985). Political myths about education reform. *Phi Delta Kappan, 66*(5), 349–351.

Ryan, K. (1970). *Don't smile until Christmas: Accounts of the first year of teaching.* Chicago: University of Chicago Press.

Schön, D.A. (1983). *The reflective practitioner: How professionals think in action.* New York: Basic Books.

Schön, D.A. (1987). *Educating the reflective practitioner: Toward a new design for teaching and learning in the professions.* San Francisco: Jossey-Bass.

Schön, D.A. (1988). Coaching reflective teaching. In P.P. Grimmett & G.L. Erickson (Eds.), *Reflection in teacher education.* New York: Teachers College Press.

Sergiovanni, T.J. (1986). Understanding reflective practice. *Journal of Curriculum and Supervision, 1*(4), 353–359.

Shavelson, R.J., & Stern, P. (1981). Research on teachers' pedagogical thoughts, judgments, decisions and behavior. *Review of Educational Research, 51,* 455–498.

Shulman, L.S. (1987). Knowledge and teaching: Foundations of the new reform. *Harvard Educational Review, 57*(1), 1–22.

Silver, C.B. (1973). *Black teachers in urban schools.* New York: Praeger.

Sizer, T. (1984). *Horace's compromize.* Boston: Houghton Mifflin.

Taylor, P.H. (1970). *How teachers plan their courses.* Slough, UK: NFER.

Tyler, R.W. (1950). *Basic principles of curriculum and instruction.* Chicago: University of Chicago Press.

Veenman, S. (1984). Perceived problems of beginning teachers. *Review of Educational Research, 54*(2), 143–178.

Zahorik, J.A. (1970). The effect of planning on teaching. *Elementary School Journal, 71,* 143–151.

Zahorik, J.A. (1975). Teachers' planning models. *Educational Leadership, 33,* 134–139.

Zumwalt, K.K. (1982). Research on teaching: Policy implications for teacher education. In A. Lieberman & M. McLaughlin (Eds.), *Policy making in education* (pp. 215–248). Chicago: NSSE.

Chapter 5

A Teacher Education Paradigm to Empower Teachers and Students

Patricia Ashton

University of Florida

INTRODUCTION

The Need for Radical Changes in Teaching

Research reports of conditions in the schools in the United States reveal a bleak landscape of demoralized teachers and disengaged students. Instruction is routine and uninspired; students, though uninvolved, are for the most part compliant. Teachers and students have negotiated a tacit agreement to expect little academic work from each other in exchange for peaceful coexistence (Cusick, 1983; Goodlad, 1984; Powell, Farrar, & Cohen, 1985; Sedlak, Wheeler, Pullin, & Cusick, 1986; Sizer, 1984).

The recent descriptions of teachers' lack of commitment to teaching suggest a serious decline in their sense of efficacy—their belief in their ability to teach and their students' ability to learn (Ashton & Webb, 1986). Experienced teachers often reflect nostalgically on the "good old days" when students cared about learning (Welsh, 1986). Their belief that students are less committed to education contributes to teachers' feelings of futility when working with difficult students. When they believe that their students cannot or will not learn, teachers exert less effort in trying to motivate uninterested students. Fearing failure and sensing their teachers' discouragement, low-achieving students tend to give up when confronted with challenging material. Thus, a debilitating cycle of defeat is established as their students' failures further weaken teachers' sense of efficacy. Commitment to education and excitement about learning will elude students and teachers as long as teachers' low efficacy attitudes remain unchallenged.

The reforms initiated to counteract the rising tide of mediocrity in schools in the United States (National Commission on Excellence in Education, 1983) have focused on raising academic standards. Lengthening the school day, competency testing of students and teachers, and increasing the academic requirements for graduation have been among the most popular means for instituting excellence in schools. Such efforts to legislate learning are doomed to fail because they do not address the attitudes and beliefs that have led students and teachers to accept mediocrity as a prevailing characteristic of their lives in schools.

Reacting to the inadequacies of the current reform initiatives, Goodlad (1984) warned that "mere refinement of conventional practice is not sufficient. We will only begin to get evidence of the potential power of pedagogy when we dare to risk and support markedly deviant classroom procedures" (p. 249). To accomplish this aim, he called for "radical breakthroughs" (p. 317).

The greatest hope for change in a profession is through the influence of new members prepared in the most sophisticated approaches available. Kuhn (1970) illustrated the power of new professionals to transform a field in his description of the process by which new paradigms emerge in science. Revolutions in scientific thought are introduced primarily by the training of a new generation of practitioners, not by the retraining of established members of a profession.

The Inadequacies of Current Teacher Education Programs

Unfortunately, existing programs of teacher education fail to prepare teachers to cope with the conditions in the schools that erode their sense of efficacy (Vaughan, 1984). Teacher education programs are typically brief, technologically impoverished, and lack conceptual clarity and programmatic consistency (Howey, 1983). Such programs are incapable of enabling teachers to resist the pressures of the school environment that force them to compromise their ideals. In spite of the high efficacy rhetoric expounded in many teacher education classes, most teacher education practices reinforce traditional beliefs and methods of teaching (Giroux, 1980; Zeichner, 1986; Zeichner & Tabachnick, 1981). Goodman's (1986b) description of the methods courses in one elementary education program illustrates how teacher education practices play a stronger role in fostering conservative attitudes in student teachers than typically assumed. Goodman found that the goal of the methods courses was to help students adapt to the existing practices in the schools. Instruction was designed to develop the teacher candidates' competence in using standardized curriculum. Students were not encouraged to develop their own materials. The conditions and practices observed in the schools were rarely questioned, and the value of the standardized curriculum was not examined. "Knowledge was usually presented in unambiguous terms with an air of finality about it" (Goodman, 1986b, pp. 344–346).

Teacher candidates regard student teaching as the most useful part of their preparation (Barnes, 1987; Sears, 1984). The prevailing practice of placing student teachers with supervising teachers without considering whether the aims and methods of the supervising teacher are consistent with the goals of the teacher education program reinforces traditional teaching practices. As Goodlad (1984) stated:

> [Casual assignment of student teachers to supervising teachers] assures perpetuation of the very things we want teacher education programs to change. The success of professional preparation . . . depends on the degree to which programs are able to separate beginners from the primitive or outworn techniques of their predecessors. If we were to set out to provide the most advanced preparation for future doctors, surely we would not intern them with those whose solution to every illness is blood-letting. (p. 316)

As Lortie (1975) noted:

> The apprenticeship-of-observation is not likely to instill a sense of the problematics of teaching. . . . [It] is an ally of continuity rather than change. (p. 67)

And, as Joyce (1975) said:

> No more effective method has ever been devised for preventing change in a social institution than to apprentice the novice to his elder. (p. 116)

Thus, teacher education—courses and student teaching—perpetuate traditional teaching practices. Radical changes in pedagogy are needed to overcome teacher and student apathy. However, the radical breakthroughs necessary to improve schooling are unlikely without similarly radical breakthroughs in the education of teachers. The purpose of this chapter is to describe a conceptual framework to guide the development of teacher education programs that can empower teacher education students to become educational leaders and innovators. The framework is grounded in a vision of education as a moral and intellectual enterprise committed to the development of excellence and equity.

TRADITIONAL PARADIGMS OF TEACHER EDUCATION

Although most teacher education programs are not based on a single, cohesive perspective, a number of distinctive orientations have been identified. Influenced by Hartnett and Naish's (1980) analysis of teacher education perspectives in Great Britain, Zeichner (1983) described four representative paradigms that dominate practice in teacher education in the United States. He defined paradigm as a "matrix of beliefs and assumptions about the nature and purposes of schooling, teaching, teachers, and their education that gives shape to specific forms of practice in teacher education" (p. 3).

According to Zeichner (1983), the predominant teacher education paradigm is behavioristic. Based on a technical production metaphor and positivistic epistemology, the behavioristic paradigm focuses on mastery of knowledge and skills identified through teacher effectiveness research. The personalistic paradigm is built on a metaphor of growth and a phenomenological epistemology that emphasizes the development of psychological maturity through attention to the self-perceived developmental needs of preservice students. The traditional-craft paradigm, an apprenticeship model, focuses on the accumulation of wisdom through the trial and error of practitioners. Underlying the inquiry-oriented paradigm is a metaphor of liberation. This paradigm emphasizes the development of preservice teachers' capacity for reflective action through an examination of the moral and political implications of their teaching. The goal of this paradigm is to enable teachers to create more humane environments for learning.

Zeichner (1983) pointed out that most teacher education programs combine elements from two or more paradigms. Although some programs purport to represent a single paradigm, they typically include faculty members committed to other paradigms. What Zeichner failed to point out is that a number of the assumptions underlying these different paradigms are incompatible with each other. Patchwork programs that combine contradictory perspectives are confusing to students and contribute to their rejection of university training (Sears, 1984). Confronted with faculty members representing contradictory perspectives, students are left alone to struggle with the inconsistencies. Most resolve the dilemma by seeking security in the utilitarian perspective of what works. Students could probably adapt to differences among individual teacher educators if programs had an overarching perspective to which all faculty adhered, but without a consistent view integrating the program students are adrift in a sea of contradictions. As Lasley (1986) warned, "The multiple perspectives leave students perplexed and dismayed. The absence of a common framework or vision engenders in many, cynicism and enmity" (p. 159).

Teachers' sense of efficacy, their belief in the ability to have an effect on student learning, is a crucial factor in their willingness to innovate (Ashton & Webb, 1986; McLaughlin & Marsh, 1978). Fragmented programs consisting of conflicting perspectives undermine the development of teachers' sense of efficacy. Baffled by seemingly irreconciliable differences, teacher candidates often cope by discounting their preparation programs (Raths, 1987). Without a consistent paradigmatic perspective from which to derive their educational aims and practices, beginning teachers are unlikely to sustain their commitment to innovative practice in the conservative environment of the school (Kirk, 1986).

DEMOCRATIC PEDAGOGY: A COMPREHENSIVE, UNIFYING PARADIGM

Zeichner (1983) criticized the "premature and often uncritical acceptance of particular paradigmatic orientations" and called for "normative debate over the proper content and focus of a teacher education program" (p. 8). This debate has begun to take the form of advocacy of guiding images of teaching to undergird the development of more conceptually consistent programs. For example, Barnes (1987) described four images that have guided development of four Michigan State teacher education programs: the Academic Learning Program, the Heterogeneous Classrooms Program, the Learning Community Program, and the Multiple Perspectives Program. Other images that have been proposed as guides for teacher education include teacher as artist (Dawe, 1984), teacher as moral craftsman (Tom, 1984), teacher as decision maker (Gideonse, 1986), teacher as political craftsman (Kohl, 1976), teacher as reflective practitioner (Zeichner & Liston, 1987), and teacher as applied scientist (Brophy & Evertson, 1976). The problem with these images is that taken individually they are too limited to guide the development of a program to prepare teachers for their multifaceted role in the complex environment of the school. For example, education in all of the themes represented in Michigan State's four programs is crucial for the development of a well-prepared teacher. Focus on one aspect of the teacher's role to the exclusion of other equally important aspects of the role will diminish the prospective teacher's potential for effectiveness. Furthermore, proliferation of such images emphasizes teacher educators' inability to identify a common vision and further fragments the profession. In his discussion of guiding conceptions, Joyce (1975) advocated the building of a "synthesis that succeeds, without sinking to an absurd eclecticism, in developing views of education and of the education of the teacher that can capitalize on the real truths that lie embedded in competing philosophies" (p. 145).

Greene's (1978) call for a new pedagogy—a democratic pedagogy—offers the synthesis that Joyce recommended. Democratic pedagogy can provide the foundation for the construction of a new paradigm capable of integrating the compatible aspects of the many perspectives and images that have been proposed within an overarching perspective consistent with the established values of American education. The objective of democratic pedagogy is "to empower persons to enact democracy. To act upon democratic values is to be responsive to consciously incarnated principles of freedom, justice, and regard for others" (pp. 70–71). Teachers effectively trained in democratic pedagogy would have characteristics derived from each of the perspectives described by Zeichner (1983): technical and inquiry skills, academic and craft knowledge, understanding of self and others, and moral and political intelligence. In Greene's (1978) words,[1] preparation in democratic pedagogy would empower teachers to

> create the kinds of conditions that move diverse young persons to take their own initiatives and move beyond what they are taught. They need to be the kinds of teachers equipped to make practical judgments on the grounds of what they have learned in the realms of theory, what they have discovered from empirical research, what they understand about children and youth, and what they understand about themselves. They need to be the kinds of teachers who can make their own thinking visible to the young, to make manifest the ways in which the modes of procedure in each domain are put to work, to submit their own judgments to the critical scrutiny of those they teach, to open perspectives, to open worlds. (p. 83)

Greene's description illustrates the comprehensiveness of the paradigm of democratic pedagogy in comparison to other paradigms. Democratic pedagogy encompasses the strengths of other perspectives in an expansive view of teacher education that has the potential to unify teacher educators and invigorate classroom life. Adoption of democratic pedagogy as the guiding conception of teacher education could provide the consistent and comprehensive perspective capable of equipping novice teachers with the moral, intellectual, and political vision needed to introduce and sustain the radical teaching practices Goodlad (1984) recommended.

---

[1] This passage, and others following by Maxine Greene, are from *Landscapes of Learning*, 1978, New York: Teachers College Press. Copyright © 1978 by Teachers College, Columbia University. All rights reserved. Reprinted by permission.

The practice of democratic pedagogy requires the development of teachers with a firm conviction of their own efficacy and their ability to empower students to develop a sense of efficacy in their lives. deCharms (1968) argued that the primary human motivation is to have an effect. The goal of democratic pedagogy is to awaken teachers and students to their potential to fulfill that need, to unleash the power of students and teachers to work together to enrich their lives, and to overcome the apathy and alienation that deaden life in schools. In the pages that follow, the assumptions and dimensions of democratic pedagogy are described.

The Epistemological Foundation of Democratic Pedagogy
Although democratic pedagogy incorporates aspects of each of the paradigms identified by Zeichner (1983), it is based on an epistemology consistent with the democratic ideal—the conception of knowledge as a social construction. This epistemology is usually associated with the personalistic and inquiry orientations and is incompatible with the conception of knowledge as given that underlies the technical and academic perspectives that students have been socialized to accept in traditional classrooms.

From years of sitting in classrooms, where the textbooks and teacher are the unquestioned authorities and the right answer is the ultimate value, teacher candidates have developed a conception of knowledge as established by experts (Britzman, 1986). Such classroom experiences lead them to a conception of the teacher as transmitter of knowledge and a conception of learning as passive absorption of information. When they begin teaching, bureaucratic constraints contribute further to their acceptance of a passive role (Sarason, 1982; Wise, 1979). Typically, their background and training have offered no countervailing experiences that could enable them to resist the influences of the bureaucracy. As Greene (1978) pointed out,

> The reality [teachers] have constructed and taken for granted allows for neither autonomy nor disagreement. They do not consider putting their objections to a test. The constructs they have inherited do not include a view of teachers as equal participants. (p. 45)

To develop a democratic pedagogy, these conceptions of knowledge and the role of the teacher must be dispelled. Teacher candidates must come to understand that the information that makes up school curriculum has been socially determined and should be subject to scrutiny in terms of its relation to the aims of democratic education. To acquire an understanding of the social construction of school knowledge, teacher candidates require experiences that enable them to discover that "teaching [is] a cultural artifact that evolves as people refine and redefine which knowledge, skills, and attitudes are important for future generations" (Tom, 1984, p. 96). As preservice students come to realize that knowledge structures in the disciplines are human inventions created to serve human interests, they will begin to understand the moral responsibility embedded in the choice of what knowledge to transmit. They will begin to recognize that the selection of the knowledge to be transmitted is a political process hidden from the view of passive learners (Keddie, 1984).

Discovering that school knowledge is socially constructed liberates teacher candidates from the mystique of the expert. When they participate in identifying taken-for-granted constructions that limit human possibilities, they become empowered to consider alternative views. For example, teacher candidates who come to understand that the concept of IQ is socially constructed and subject to controversy are liberated from a rigid acceptance of a student's IQ score as a reification of the student's human potential. They will be less likely to succumb to a sense of helplessness in working with students who have low IQ scores.

Thus, the conception of knowledge implicit in democratic pedagogy would liberate preservice students from the constraints the conception of knowledge as given imposes. Liberated from a passive approach to knowledge, they would be empowered to free their students from "the unwarranted control of unjustified belief, unsupportable attitudes, and the paucity of abilities which can prevent [them] from completely taking charge of [their lives]" (Siegel, 1980, cited in Zeichner & Liston, 1987).

Practice of democratic pedagogy assumes that teachers are not inextricably trapped, impotent victims of the school culture. Awareness of the construction of school knowledge empowers teachers to influence the school curriculum. As Grant and Sleeter (1985) concluded from a three-year ethnographic study of a junior high school in the midwest, "teacher work is determined as much by teachers themselves—that is, their conceptions of society and education—as it is by factors in their workplace" (p. 219). The epistemology undergirding democratic pedagogy implies that "individuals are not 'taken over' by cultures. They can both contribute toward, and be influenced by them in a dialectical process" (Woods, 1983, p. 77).

The Moral Dimension of Democratic Pedagogy
The technical paradigm's dominance in teacher education has led to excessive dependence on empirical data as the criterion of educational

effectiveness. As policy makers have turned increasingly to empirical research to identify effective educational methods, questions of educational aims have been avoided. The fragmentation and emphasis on methods in teacher education reflect the lack of a moral vision to guide the preparation of teachers.

The influence that teachers have over students' lives creates an inherently moral responsibility (Tom, 1984). However, studies in schools indicate that many teachers shrink from this responsibility. Powell, Farrar, and Cohen (1985) concluded from their observations in high schools that teachers "abdicate responsibility for pushing all students to learn and to care about learning" (p. 310). Blaming students for their failure, many teachers settle for a smoothly running classroom and disengaged students. From their longitudinal study of a desegregated and mainstreamed junior high school, Grant and Sleeter (1985) concluded that most of the teachers they observed

> did not seem dedicated to seeing that the students attain their full potential in life, to providing students with the knowledge and skills with which to change society so that it could benefit oppressed people more, or to refine their teaching skills continually to help the students rise above their present life circumstances. (p. 218)

Grant and Sleeter attributed the teachers' apathy to their personal backgrounds and training and their unquestioned acceptance of the conception of society and education implicit in the current organization of schools.

Recognition of the socially constructed nature of teaching inevitably raises the question of the human purposes that underlie the process of social construction. This question brings to the fore the necessity of a moral dimension in teacher education (Tom, 1984). As long as the circumstances of life in schools are taken for granted and accepted as "the way it spozed [sic] to be" (Herndon, 1968), the moral implications of the teaching situation can be ignored (Greene, 1978). Becoming aware that authority relations in the school, standards for behavior, selection of curriculum, expectations for learners, and uses of testing are socially determined awakens one to the moral choices embedded in the school reality (Tom, 1984).

The moral sensibility of preservice teachers must be aroused to prevent them from succumbing to the utilitarian perspective that ignores the moral responsibility that they bear for student achievement. According to Greene (1978):

> It [is] important for teachers, no matter what their specialty, to be clear about how they ground their own values, their own conceptions of the

good and of the possible. . . . They have to . . . overcome their own submergence in the habitual, even in what they conceive to be the virtuous, and ask the "why" with which learning and moral reasoning begin. (pp. 46–47)

A first step in raising the moral consciousness of teacher candidates should be to provide them with a supportive context in which they are challenged to articulate their moral philosophy of teaching and to evaluate their teaching in terms of its consistency with their moral philosophy. Such exploration of their values and their implications for teaching should help sensitize teacher candidates to the moral power of teaching and contribute to the development of a strong sense of efficacy.

Guided by teacher educators who engage them in examination of the moral dimension of teaching, novice teachers could begin to model this orientation with their own students. Students are most likely to be engaged when their teachers are actively involved. As Greene (1978) stated: "The young are most likely to be stirred to learn when they are challenged by teachers who themselves are learning, who are breaking with what they have too easily taken for granted, who are creating their own moral lives" (p. 51).

The Academic Dimension of Democratic Pedagogy

Zeichner (1983) mentioned the academic paradigm but omitted it from extended discussion on the grounds that adherents of all teacher education paradigms accept the critical role of liberal education in teacher preparation. In contrast, the commission reports have consistently concluded that teachers' preparation in the liberal arts and sciences is inadequate. In addition, recent critics have blamed teacher educators for students' unsatisfactory performance on tests of academic knowledge (Hirsch, 1987; Ravitch & Finn, 1987). These critics have attributed students' ignorance of the basic facts of the United States' cultural heritage to teacher educators' emphasis on skills rather than content. Hirsch traced "the decline of teaching cultural literacy" to the "fragmented" and "content-neutral" curriculum that has resulted from education's dominance by John Dewey's "faulty educational theories" (pp. xiii & 18–19).

To increase the academic knowledge of teachers, many of the reports have recommended that teacher education programs require a liberal arts and sciences major as a prerequisite for admission to a postbaccalaureate program of teacher education. This recommendation is unlikely to improve teaching significantly. Simply adding teacher education to a liberal arts degree program is not likely to enable teachers to integrate their liberal arts background into their pedagogical repertoire. Development of democratic pedagogy requires that teachers are thoroughly grounded in the cultural knowledge needed to empower their students to assume the social responsibilities of life in a democratic society (Dewey, 1909). To fulfill this responsibility, teachers need a dynamic understanding of the cultural heritage of the United States. American high school students' inability to answer questions about literature and history is due more to the failure of teachers to ground cultural information in a meaningful context than to students' lack of access to the information (Welsh, 1986). To enable teacher candidates to develop this dynamic understanding of academic knowledge, liberal arts preparation and teacher education must be integrated. Courses in the liberal arts and sciences as currently conceived do not enable teacher education candidates to think about their subject matter in ways that empower them to transform their knowledge of the subject into meaningful learning experiences for their students. A conception of education as transmission of knowledge predominates in the liberal arts curriculum (Finn & Ravitch, 1984). As Boyer's (1987) observations in college classrooms revealed,

> . . . students are rarely provided the opportunity to question, to challenge, to explore their doubts, introduce new assumptions, and have such contributions carefully critiqued. These are the conditions out of which genuine learning will occur. (pp. 158–159)

Shulman (1987) described the conception of academic knowledge needed for effective teaching:

> [The teacher] must understand the structures of subject matter, the principles of conceptual organization, and the principles of inquiry that help answer two kinds of questions in each field: What are the important ideas and skills in this domain? and How are new ideas added and deficient ones dropped by those who produce knowledge in this area? That is, what are the rules and procedures of good scholarship or inquiry? (p. 9)

Development of democratic pedagogy requires an integrated program of baccalaureate and postbaccalaureate studies that include liberal arts courses designed to enable novice teachers to construct usable conceptions of the subjects they will teach. Postponing teacher education until the postbaccalaureate years and overlaying it on a traditional liberal arts degree leaves teacher educators with too little time to overcome the inadequacies of 16 years of passive schooling.

The Technical Dimension of Democratic Pedagogy

The dominant orientation in teacher education in the United States has been technical, with emphasis on the passive adoption and demonstration of teaching skills believed to be related to student achievement. Grounded in a positivistic epistemology, behavioristic psychology, and the cult of efficiency (Callahan, 1962) of the early 20th century, this orientation has gained renewed vigor as state departments of education have moved increasingly to performance measurement systems of teacher evaluation based on process-product research.

The technical orientation gains further power from the practical perspective that characterizes the thinking of most students entering preservice programs. Teacher candidates want to know how: how to discipline, how to motivate, how to teach (Sears, 1984). Fears about whether they can control their students' classroom behavior increase their technical concerns. Teacher education faculty and courses that fail to address these concerns are typically viewed by students as too theoretical and irrelevant (Sears, 1984).

In the past, the methods of teacher education have reinforced the teacher candidates' practical perspective. Field experiences focused their attention on the need to "fit into the conservative and established patterns of traditional school practice" (Goodman, 1986a, p. 109). Seminars addressed their control concerns "focusing on how to teach rather than why and what" (Goodman, 1986a, p. 111). In sum, programs produced technicians prepared to perpetuate traditional teaching practices.

The democratic pedagogy advocated in this chapter requires rejection of the epistemological assumptions of the technical paradigm that imply that prescriptions for effective teaching can be derived from the demonstration of relationships between teacher skills and pupil achievement. Democratic pedagogy is based on the assumption that justification of teaching practices must be founded on moral principles. Technology, however, can be useful as a means to ethical educational ends. In this sense, education for the practice of democratic pedagogy includes development of expertise in the technologies of teaching because mastery of alternative technologies equips teachers with skills that can be helpful in achieving the normative aims of education.

Technical training is of greatest value during the early stages of teacher education. When used in appropriate contexts, process-product research can suggest strategies for organizing classrooms and managing students' behavior (see Ross & Kyle, 1987). Learning these strategies can help allay the survival fears that preoccupy most novice teachers (Fuller, 1974; Woods, 1985). However, teacher education for democratic pedagogy does not stop with technical training. It requires students to consider the moral implications of the technologies they master.

The Inquiry Dimension of Democratic Pedagogy

The limitations of the technical perspective can be seen in the rising discontent with the failure of professional knowledge to solve the problems of education. For example, in their review of research on teacher education, Lanier and Little (1986) concluded that because of its complex, social nature teacher education "is apt to be advanced least by adherence to the classic natural science modes of inquiry" (p. 528). Similarly, Schön (1983) concluded that the problems of education are too fuzzy and ill-defined to lend themselves to technical problem solving:

> [From the technical perspective] professional practice is a process of problem solving. . . . In real world practice, problems do not present themselves to the practitioner as givens. They must be constructed from the materials of problematic situations which are puzzling, troubling, and uncertain. (p. 40)

Recognizing the inadequacies of the technical paradigm, Zeichner (1983) emphasized the examination of the moral and political implications of teaching in his conception of the inquiry paradigm. It should be noted, however, that numerous inquiry approaches to education have been proposed (Tom, 1985). Some of these models of inquiry are based on technical assumptions (e.g., Cruickshank's [1987] reflective teaching). Consistent with Zeichner's inquiry paradigm, the inquiry dimension of democratic pedagogy incorporates the assumptions of the social construction of knowledge, the intrinsic relationship between empirical and normative analysis, and the necessity to link knowledge and action (Tom, 1985). These assumptions are implicit in Schön's (1983) description of the reflective practitioner:

> As teachers attempted to become reflective practitioners, they would feel constrained by and would push against the rule-governed system of the school, and in doing so they would be pushing against the theory of knowledge which underlies the school. Not only would they struggle against the rigid order of lesson plans, schedules, isolated classrooms, and objective measures of performance; they would also question and criticize the fundamental idea of the school as a place for the progressive transmission of measured doses of privileged knowledge. . . . In a school supportive of reflective teaching, teachers would challenge the prevailing knowledge structure. Their on-the-spot experiments would affect not only

the routines of teaching practice but the central values and principles of the institution. (pp. 334–335)

The Political Dimension of Democratic Pedagogy

Without political skills that empower them to act on their critical analyses of teaching, preservice teachers' development of inquiry and moral perspectives will simply increase their dissatisfaction with the profession of teaching. If teachers are to implement a democratic pedagogy, they must come to understand the cultures of teaching (Feiman-Nemser & Floden, 1986) and the role of politics in education. They must develop skill in political action and decision making that will empower them to sustain their high efficacy attitudes and their commitment to challenging teaching, and they must learn to establish strong, supportive relationships with colleagues, administrators, and the families in the school community.

Studies of beginning teachers reveal immense barriers to the goal of enabling novice teachers to become political agents for change. Beginning teachers are rapidly socialized into the school culture and abandon their idealism for custodial attitudes of impersonality, pessimism, and watchful distrust (Hoy, 1968). The conditions of teaching and the hidden pedagogy of classroom experience diminish the enthusiasm of the beginning teacher (Denscombe, 1982; Hargreaves, 1972). However, mounting evidence reveals that disillusion and subordination to the system are not inevitable. Some beginning teachers manage to resist the conservative influences of the school environment. In his study of the socialization of student teachers, Lacey (1977) discovered that some novice teachers succeeded in introducing change into their teaching situations. By using a strategy Lacey called *strategic redefinition,* these beginning teachers resisted the institution's effort to change them and influenced individuals with legitimate power to accept their interpretation of what should occur in classrooms. Kohl (1976) outlined some practical insights to help teachers become successful political activists.

If teacher preparation helped to expose the moral injustices inherent in traditional schooling practices and fostered the development of political skills of strategic redefinition, novice teachers could be empowered to resist the conservative influence of the school as a workplace. To achieve this goal, teacher educators must recognize that empowerment is a developmental process. In an ethnographic interview study of emerging citizen leaders, Kieffer (1984) identified four stages of empowerment that evolved over the course of several years. He concluded that "empowerment is not a commodity to be acquired, but a transforming process constructed through action. . . . Reflective experience is the irreducible source of growth. Individuals must learn to overcome internalized expectations of helplessness" (p. 27).

Kieffer's description of the evolution of empowerment suggests that if teacher education programs are to empower their graduates to improve education, programs must be based on a developmental model that responds to the growing capabilities of prospective teachers. A hierarchy of increasingly proactive experiences must be included in the curriculum that require students to confront low efficacy beliefs and critically analyze the social and political nature of teaching and the conditions in schools that frustrate and disempower teachers. To counteract feelings of helplessness, teacher candidates need to learn skills of collaboration and political action that will enable them to participate in educational decision making. Ultimately, they need to engage in action that enables them to overcome the role conflicts and strains that lead to burnout.

The Personalistic Dimension of Democratic Pedagogy

As the discussion of its epistemology and moral and political dimensions suggests, the practice of democratic pedagogy requires psychological self-awareness and social and political insights that few entering preservice students possess. Understanding the process of the social construction of knowledge depends on an awareness that knowledge about effective teaching cannot be discovered with absolute certainty from direct experience but rather consists of reasonable conjectures based on the evaluation of evidence derived from study, experimentation, and reflection. In contrast, most college students view knowledge as absolute and derived directly from experience (Kitchener, 1986).

Teacher education programs that fail to recognize the developmental limitations of students with regard to their understanding of the social construction of knowledge are unlikely to have a long-term impact. Preservice students expect to learn what works in their teacher education classes. They anticipate that they will learn to teach by teaching. Instruction based on inquiry or moral perspectives that does not have direct application to the classroom will be dismissed as too theoretical, too abstract, too liberal, or irrelevant (Feiman-Nemser, 1987; Lortie, 1975; Sears, 1984). To enable prospective teachers to construct an understanding of the epistemology undergirding democratic pedagogy and the dimensions that define it, teacher education programs must be developmental. They must begin with entering students' technical orientation and gradually challenge their subjectively reasonable beliefs (Fenstermacher, 1979). If the program does not challenge their utilitarian perspective and demonstrate the inadequacies of the technical paradigm, teacher candidates will in all likelihood graduate with the same orientation with which they entered.

Inducing change in students' conceptions of the nature of knowledge is a gradual process. Longitudinal research has shown only limited growth toward an understanding of the social construction of knowledge during a one-to-three year interval (Kitchener, 1986). Parallels between development of reflective judgment and development of other logical structures (Kohlberg, 1979; Piaget, 1972) suggest that students must be exposed to experiences that provoke them to question the adequacy of their technical orientation. Faced with the dissonance created by the conflicts between their experiences and their beliefs, students are motivated to restructure their understanding at a more sophisticated level. Although research on the process of inducing change in epistemological assumptions is just beginning, it is evident that an extended period of teacher preparation is needed to stimulate the quality of thinking essential for democratic pedagogy.

Recognizing the need to adapt teacher education programs to students' level of understanding, Thies-Sprinthall and Sprinthall (1987) recommended a two-track system: a highly structured, didactic program for students at a concrete level of development and a more abstract and inductive program for students functioning at a higher level of development. Social interaction between students at different levels of development has been shown to be an important factor in inducing growth (Rest, 1986). Therefore, segregation of students into a two-track system deprives the more concrete students of a major source of developmental stimulation—interaction with peers who have a more abstract view of teaching.

In sum, a teacher education program designed to foster democratic pedagogy must gradually involve students in probing examination of their personal beliefs about the nature of teaching and learning. The developmental limitations of students entering teacher education programs indicate that learning to think like a professional teacher is a developmental process requiring time for reflection and growth. Short-term programs, like the Master's programs recommended by the Holmes Group (1986), are unlikely to offer sufficient time to induce the level of development needed to overcome preservice teachers' epistemological attraction to the utilitarian perspective.

PRELIMINARY EFFORTS TOWARD A DEMOCRATIC PEDAGOGY

A number of innovative practices have been proposed that could help preservice teachers develop a democratic pedagogy. Woods (1985) recommended training in the use of ethnography because it provides teachers with insight into themselves and the process of education and is a means of increasing teachers' sense of efficacy. Greene's (1978) use of aesthetics and literature to illuminate the purposes and processes of education offers an example of how liberal arts courses could sensitize students to the power of education to give life meaning and direction. Tesconi (1972) proposed the use of phenomenological analysis to intensify students' understanding of themselves and others, to deepen their sense of personal responsibility and create an impassioned approach to learning. Schon (1987) outlined a practicum approach to the development of reflective teaching. Through the assistance of a coach who demonstrates, advises, and criticizes, the novice practitioner practices reflection in action in laboratory settings that simulate and simplify real-world practice. Goodman (1986a) described an early field experience that encouraged students to examine critically their experience in schools and fostered their sense of efficacy by using the field experience as a laboratory setting where they experimented with creative approaches to curriculum development..Ross (1987) described the writing of theory-to-practice papers as a means of stimulating reflective thinking. Action research has been widely recommended as a particularly effective means of raising teachers' consciousness regarding their potential as an agent for change (Carr & Kemmis, 1983; Goswami & Stillman, 1987; Nixon, 1981).

Of programs described in the teacher education literature, the elementary school student teaching program at the University of Wisconsin, Madison, comes closest to embodying the democratic pedagogy described in this chapter and incorporates a number of the aforementioned strategies, including ethnography and action research (Zeichner & Liston, 1987). In this program, elements of the technical and moral craft perspectives are integrated in an overarching inquiry paradigm. The intent of the program is

> to develop the desire and ability to assume greater roles in determining the direction of classroom and school affairs according to purposes of which they are aware and which can be justified on moral and educational grounds, as well as on instrumental grounds. (pp. 25–26)

Unfortunately, two studies (Tabachnick & Zeichner, 1984; Zeichner & Grant, 1981) that examined the effect of the student teaching program found that the program had little effect on the students' perspectives toward teaching.

As suggested in the previous section, changing students' epistemological assumptions is a developmental process. Short-term efforts of a semester or even a year's duration do not provide sufficient time for the experimentation and reflection needed to induce significant changes.

The prospect of stimulating enduring change is further diminished when these efforts are attempted in the context of programs characterized by "ideological eclecticism" and "structural fragmentation" (Zeichner & Liston, 1987, p. 43). A variety of strategies have potential for helping preservice teachers become adept in democratic pedagogy; however, they must be integrated within a developmental program with ideological consistency and a coherent structural framework.

CONCLUSION

The conditions of apathy and alienation in the schools will worsen unless dramatic changes in teachers and teacher preparation occur. According to Haberman (1984), by the end of the decade, "in almost every major city of over 500,000 population, the majority of students will be those now defined as minority, poverty, handicapped" (pp. 498–499). At the same time that the school-age minority population is exploding, the number of minority teachers is declining. In 1983, the National Center for Educational Statistics reported that 91% of new graduates qualified to teach were white, nonhispanic, 6% were black, and 1.7% were hispanic (Howey, 1986). As the ethnic background and socioeconomic levels of teachers and students become increasingly divergent, relations between teachers and students will become increasingly difficult. As Grant and Sleeter (1987) pointed out, the personal backgrounds of white working- and middle-class teachers and teacher educators limit their understanding of the needs and perspectives of minority students. This lack of understanding contributes to the development of low efficacy attitudes that allow teachers to blame these students for their failure and to abandon efforts to help them overcome their difficult circumstances. Current teacher education programs, with their paradigmatic eclecticism and fragmented faculties, are incapable of preparing teachers to maintain a strong sense of efficacy in the face of the obstacles these demographic conditions will impose. Without teachers with strong efficacy attitudes, the life chances of growing numbers of minority students will be limited by the utilitarian perspective embodied in the recent wave of standards-raising reforms (Sedlak, Wheeler, Pullin, & Cusick, 1986). A paradigm for teacher preparation is needed that has the potential to unify teacher educators and empower teachers and students. Democratic pedagogy, with its emphasis on the development of a moral and intellectual and political vision of teaching, could invigorate teachers' and students' sense of efficacy.

I am concerned that the paradigm of democratic pedagogy as a design for teacher education will be dismissed as naive and unworkable.

Admittedly, teacher education alone cannot remedy the debilitating conditions in the schools. Without more equitable economic and social conditions, teachers' ability to empower their students will continue to be seriously restricted; without more equitable rewards for teaching, teachers will continue to experience dissatisfaction with the profession; without reduced student-teacher ratios and more planning time, teachers will be unable to devote much time to reflection and experimentation. Admittedly, the paradigm requires an unprecedented degree of collaboration among teacher educators as well as between teacher educators and liberal arts faculty. Lanier and Little (1986) sketched an unfavorable view of teacher educators as largely rigid, shallow, anti-intellectual, and conforming—in sum, sharing their students' utilitarian values. If Lanier and Little's description of teacher educators is accurate, perhaps teacher education for democratic pedagogy is unworkable. Certainly, the past failures of teacher educators to improve teacher practices offer little reason to be hopeful, but I remain optimistic. The current climate of educational reform offers an opportunity for teacher educators to collaborate to develop programs that empower prospective teachers to improve educational practice, and our understanding of needed changes is greater than ever before. As Vaughan (1984) advised,

> If teacher educators can provide prospective teachers with a more complete and accurate understanding of what to expect in schools and why, they will possess a basis for working in a positive fashion for improving those conditions. Without such content in teacher education, new teachers will likely be surprised, confused, frustrated, and maybe even bitter as they undertake their beginning years of teaching. (p. 5)

If radical changes in teaching and learning in schools do not occur, the future of democracy in the United States is in jeopardy. Greene (1978) warned:

> Nor is democracy conceivable in a society permeated by indifference, frozen in technological language, and rooted in inequities. So the concern of teacher educators must remain normative, critical, and even political. Neither the teachers' colleges nor the schools can change the social order. Neither colleges nor schools can legislate democracy. But something can be done to empower some teachers-to-be to reflect upon their own life situations, to speak out in their own voices about the lacks that must be repaired, the possibilities to be acted upon in the name of what they deem decent, humane, and just. (p. 71)

REFERENCES

Ashton, P., & Webb, R. (1986). *Making a difference: Teachers' sense of efficacy and student achievement.* White Plains, NY: Longman.

Barnes, H. (1987). The conceptual basis for thematic teacher education programs. *Journal of Teacher Education, 38,* 13–18.

Boyer, E. (1987). *College. The undergraduate experience in America.* New York: Harper & Row.

Britzman, D.P. (1986). Cultural myths in the making of a teacher: Biography and social structure in teacher education. *Harvard Educational Review, 56*(4), 442–456.

Brophy, J., & Evertson, C. (1976). *Learning from teaching.* Boston: Allyn & Bacon.

Callahan, R. E. (1962). *Education and the cult of efficiency.* Chicago: The University of Chicago Press.

Carr, W., & Kemmis, S. (1983). *Becoming critical: Education, knowledge, and action research.* London: Falmer Press.

Cruickshank, D.R. (1987). *Reflective teaching: The preparation of students of teaching.* Reston, VA: Association of Teacher Educators.

Cusick, P.A. (1983). *The egalitarian ideal and the American high school. Studies of three schools.* New York: Longman.

Dawe, H.A. (1984). Teaching: A performing art. *Phi Delta Kappan, 66*(7), 548–552.

deCharms, R. (1968). *Personal causation.* New York: Academic Press.

Denscombe, M. (1982). The hidden pedagogy and its implications for teacher training. *British Journal of Sociology of Education, 3,* 249–265.

Dewey, J. (1909). *Moral principles in education.* Boston: Houghton Mifflin.

Feiman-Nemser, S. (1987, April). *Ed. Psych is not Ed. Psych is not Ed. Psych: Comparing the content and pedagogy of two foundations courses.* Paper presented at the meeting of the American Educational Research Association, Washington, DC.

Feiman-Nemser, S., & Floden, R. (1986). The cultures of teaching. In M.C. Wittrock (Ed.), *Handbook of research on teaching* (3rd ed., pp. 505–526). New York: Macmillan.

Fenstermacher, G.D. (1979). A philosophical consideration of recent research on teacher effectiveness. In L. Shulman (Ed.), *Review of Research in Education, Vol. 6* (pp. 157–185). Itasca, IL: Peacock.

Finn, C., Jr., & Ravitch, D. (1984). Conclusions and recommendations: High expectations and disciplined efforts. In C. Finn, Jr., D. Ravitch, & R. Fancher (Eds.), *Against mediocrity. The humanities in America's high schools* (pp. 237–262). New York: Holmes & Meier.

Fuller, F.A. (1974). Conceptual framework for a personalized teacher educational program. *Theory into Practice, 13,* 112–122.

Gideonse, H. (1986). Guiding images for teaching and teacher education. In T.J. Lasley (Ed.), *The dynamics of change in teacher education. Vol. 1: Background papers from the National Commission for Excellence in Teacher Education* (pp. 187–198). Washington, DC: American Association of Colleges for Teacher Education.

Giroux, H. (1980). Teacher education and the ideology of social control. *Journal of Education, 162,* 5–27.

Goodlad, J.I. (1984). *A place called school.* New York: McGraw-Hill.

Goodman, J. (1986a). Making early field experience meaningful: A critical approach. *Journal of Education for Teaching, 12*(2), 109–125.

Goodman, J. (1986b). University education courses and the professional preparation of teachers: A descriptive analysis. *Teaching and Teacher Education, 2*(4), 341–353.

Goswami, D., & Stillman, P. (Eds.). (1987). *Reclaiming the classroom: Teacher research as an agency for change.* Upper Montclair, NJ: Boynton/Cook.

Grant, C.A., & Sleeter, C.E. (1987). Who determines teacher work? The debate continues. *Teaching and Teacher Education, 3*(1), 61–64.

Greene, M. (1978). *Landscapes of learning.* New York: Teachers College Press.

Haberman, M. (1984). Teacher education in 2000. *Education and Urban Society, 16*(4), 497–509.

Hargreaves, D.H. (1972). Staffroom relationships. *New Society, 32,* 434–437.

Hartnett, A., & Naish, M. (1983). Technicians or social bandits? Some moral and political issues in the education of teachers. In P. Woods (Ed.), *Teacher strategies* (pp. 254–274). London: Croom Helm.

Herndon, J. (1968). *The way it spozed to be.* New York: Simon & Schuster.

Hirsch, E.D., Jr. (1987). *Cultural literacy. What every American needs to know.* Boston: Houghton Mifflin.

Holmes Group. (1986). *Tomorrow's teachers: A report of the Holmes Group.* East Lansing, MI: Author.

Howey, K. (1983). Teacher education: An overview. In K. Howey & W. Gardner (Eds.), *Teacher education: A look ahead* (pp. 6–37). New York: Longman.

Howey, K. (1986). The next generation of teacher education programs. In T. J. Lasley (Ed.), *The dynamics of change in teacher education. Vol. 1. Background papers from the National Commission for Excellence in Teacher Education* (pp. 161–185). Washington, DC: American Association of Colleges for Teacher Education.

Hoy, W. (1968). The influence of experience on the beginning teacher. *Journal of Educational Research, 66,* 89–93.

Joyce, B. (1975). Conceptions of man and their implications for teacher education. In K. Ryan (Ed.), *Teacher education. Seventy-fourth yearbook of the National Society for the Study of Education* (pp. 111–145). Chicago: University of Chicago Press.

Keddie, N. (1984). Classroom knowledge. In A. Hargreaves & P. Woods (Eds.), *Classrooms and staffrooms: The sociology of teachers and teaching* (pp. 108–122). Milton Keynes: Open University Press.

Kieffer, C.H. (1984). Citizen improvement: A developmental perspective. In J. Rappaport, C. Swift, & R. Hess (Eds.), *Studies in improvement: Steps toward understanding and action* (pp. 9–36). New York: Haworth.

Kirk, D. (1986). Beyond the limits of theoretical discourse in teacher education: Towards a critical pedagogy. *Teaching and Teacher Education, 2*(2), 155–168.

Kitchener, K. (1986). The reflective judgment model: Characteristics, evidence, and measurement. In R.A. Mines & K.S. Kitchener (Eds.), *Adult cognitive development. Methods and models* (pp. 76–91). New York: Praeger.

Kohl, H. (1976). *On teaching.* New York: Schocken Books.

Kohlberg, L. (1979). *Meaning and measurement of moral development.* Worcester, MA: Clark University Press.

Kuhn, T. (1970). *The structure of scientific revolutions.* Chicago: University of Chicago Press.

Lacey, C. (1977). *The socialization of teachers.* London: Methuen.

Lanier, J., & Little, J. (1986). Research on teacher education. In M. C. Wittrock (Ed.), *Handbook of research on teaching* (3rd ed., pp. 527–569). New York: Macmillan.

Lasley, T.J. (Ed.). (1986). *The dynamics of change in teacher education. Vol. 1. Background papers from the National Commission for Excellence in Teacher Education.* Washington, DC: American Association of Colleges for Teacher Education.

Lortie, D. (1975). *Schoolteacher.* Chicago: University of Chicago Press.

McLaughlin, M.W., & Marsh, D.D. (1978). Staff development and school change. *Teachers College Record, 80*(1), 69–94.

National Commission on Excellence in Education. (1983). *A nation at risk: The imperative for educational reform.* Washington, DC: U.S. Government Printing Office.

Nixon, J. (Ed.). (1981). *A teachers' guide to action research. Evaluation, enquiry, and development in the classroom.* London: Grant McIntyre.

Piaget, J. (1972). Intellectual evolution from adolescence to adulthood. *Human Development, 15*, 1-12.

Powell, A.G., Farrar, E., & Cohen, D.K. (1985). *The shopping mall high school. Winners and losers in the educational marketplace.* Boston: Houghton Mifflin.

Raths, J. (1987). An alternative view of the evaluation of teacher education programs. In M. Haberman & J.M. Backus (Eds.), *Advances in teacher education* (Vol. 3, pp. 202-217). Norwood, NJ: Ablex.

Ravitch, D., & Finn, C., Jr. (1987). *What do our 17-year-olds know? A report on the First National Assessment of History and Literature.* New York: Harper & Row.

Rest, J. (1986). Moral development in young adults. In R.A. Mines & K.S. Kitchener (Eds.), *Adult cognitive development. Methods and models* (pp. 92-111). New York: Praeger.

Ross, D. (1987, April). *Teaching teacher effectiveness research to students: First steps in developing a reflective approach to teaching.* Paper presented at the American Educational Research Association, Washington, DC.

Ross, D.D., & Kyle, D.W. (1987). Helping preservice teachers learn to use teacher effectiveness research. *Journal of Teacher Education, 38,* 40-44.

Sarason, S. (1982). *Problems of change and the culture of the school.* New York: Allyn & Bacon.

Schön, D. (1983). *The reflective practitioner: How professionals think in action.* New York: Basic Books.

Schön, D. (1987). *Educating the reflective practitioner: Toward a new design for teaching and learning in the professions.* San Francisco: Jossey-Bass.

Sears, J. T. (1984). *A critical ethnography of teacher education programs at Indiana University: An inquiry into the perceptions of students and faculty regarding quality and effectiveness.* Unpublished doctoral dissertation, Indiana University, Bloomington.

Sedlak, M., Wheeler, C.W., Pullin, D.C., & Cusick, P.A. (1986). *Selling students short. Classroom bargains and academic reforms in the American high school.* New York: Teachers College Press.

Shulman, L. (1987). Knowledge and teaching: Foundations of the new reform. *Harvard Educational Review, 57*(1), 1-22.

Siegel, H. (1980). Critical thinking as an educational ideal. *Educational Forum, 45,* 7-23.

Sizer, T. (1984). *Horace's compromise: The dilemma of the American high school.* Boston: Houghton Mifflin.

Tabachnick, B.R., & Zeichner, K. (1984). The impact of the student teaching experience on the development of teacher perspectives. *Journal of Teacher Education, 35,* 28-42.

Tesconi, C., Jr., & Morris, V. (1972). *The anti-man culture. Bureautechnocracy and the schools.* Urbana, IL: University of Illinois.

Thies-Sprinthall, L., & Sprinthall, N.A. (1987). Preservice teachers as adult learners: A new framework for teacher education. In M. Haberman & J.M. Backus (Eds.), *Advances in teacher education* (Vol. 3, pp. 35-56). Norwood, NJ: Ablex.

Tom, A. (1984). *Teaching as a moral craft.* White Plains, NY: Longman.

Tom, A. (1985). Inquiring into inquiry-oriented teacher education. *Journal of Teacher Education, 36*(5), 35-44.

Vaughan, J. (1984). Knowledge resources for improving the content of preservice teacher education. *Journal of Teacher Education, 35*(4), 3-7.

Welsh, P. (1986). *Tales out of school. A teacher's candid account from the front lines of the American high school today.* New York: Penguin.

Wise, A. (1979). *Legislated learning: The bureaucratization of the American classroom.* Berkeley: University of California Press.

Woods, P. (1983). *Sociology and the school.* London: Routledge & Kegan Paul.

Woods, P. (1985). Sociology, ethnography, and teacher practice. *Teaching and Teacher Education, 1*(1), 51–62.

Zeichner, K. (1983). Alternative paradigms of teacher education. *Journal of Teacher Education, 34*(3), 3–9.

Zeichner, K. (1986). Individual and institutional influences on the development of teacher perspectives. In J. Raths & L. Katz (Eds.), *Advances in teacher education* (Vol. 2, pp. 135–163). Norwood, NJ: Ablex.

Zeichner, K., & Grant, C. (1981). Biography and social structure in the socialization of student teachers. *Journal of Education for Teaching, 1,* 198–314.

Zeichner, K., & Liston, D. (1987). Teaching student teachers to reflect. *Harvard Educational Review, 57*(1), 23–48.

Zeichner, K., & Tabachnick, B.R. (1981). Are the effects of university teacher education "washed out" by school experience? *Journal of Teacher Education, 32*(3), 7–11.

Chapter 6
The Beginning Teacher as Theory Maker: Meanings for Teacher Education*

Patricia M. Copa

University of Minnesota

Susan sat on a table in the back of her seventh grade math classroom. She ran her fingers through her tousled brown hair and contemplated the events of the day.

A beaming brown face appeared through the open door. "Hi, Ms. King. Can I come in here this hour?" Susan sighed, "Not today, Tanya. I need some peace and quiet. Close the door, will you? Thanks."

Susan's principal had called her "variable" (inconsistent) that morning, and it had nagged at her all day. It made it hard for her to teach math while dealing with the minute-to-minute crises of her noisy, crowded, inner-city classroom. She felt she had to reconcile in her own mind why she seemed to react so strongly to some of the things the kids did while brushing off other antics.

"It isn't not being able to put things in an order of seriousness. It's worse than that because you don't know everything that's going to happen. So, I think that's kind of what happened to me. At the beginning, I was going on these other things and those weren't that big a deal to other people and they didn't get dealt with much. So I just kind of stopped having things dealt with by the administration—if it's not something that's just ruining the class at the moment and it's something I feel I

* This study was supported in part by a grant from the Teaching and Learning Section of the National Institute of Education. Grant No. NIE-B-81-0190.

can ignore. Even when a kid hit me once, I just went to the social worker and wasn't even going to report it to administration. Well, that was different—they just went nuts about that.

In my head, I haven't been variable, and just to be called that is hard. It's like being hit and the person walks away and you can't do anything."

Each new teacher enters the classroom more or less a stranger in a strange land. The suitcases he or she carries are filled with articles from the old country, the familiar land just left. There are guides with innovative techniques and schema for teaching everything from punctuation to critical thinking. There are stories of good teachers propelling reluctant students toward learning in spite of themselves. There are chronicles of teaching episodes drawn from various classrooms experienced over the previous 20 years, from television and movies, and from Dickens and Holt. Finally, there are pictures of students, eager and reticent, large and small, girls and boys, perhaps "challenging," but never incorrigible.

What makes the situation of the teacher traveler different from others who have gone to strange places before is that he or she is expected to become governor of part of this new land. Furthermore, the job explicitly involves *transforming* the inhabitants, often employing whatever the stranger carries with him or her on arrival. What the natives should become is found in the guides, pictures, chronicles, and stories of the stranger brought from the unfamiliar land.

However, extending the analogy a bit further, as might be expected, the inhabitants seldom accept this transformation passively. In fact, they have suitcases of their own filled with artifacts from their own land(s). In addition, the territory itself may be different from the traveler's home country and may have idiosyncrasies that were not anticipated. Its higher authorities may put pressures on the stranger to do things that conflict with the ideas from the other land.

The ways that beginning teachers approach their new worlds—the classrooms in which students are expected to learn—the problems these new educators encounter and the actions they employ, have been the focus of much concern and study over the past several decades. In times such as the present, when special interest is directed toward improving the form and substance of education, it is not surprising that the new teacher is targeted for particular attention. Recommendations from local, state, and national study commissions reflect concomitant concern for the welfare and tenure of new educators as well as for quality educational experiences for their students. However, what has undoubtedly been a sincere desire to make conditions better for both new teachers and their students has tended to rely on a dominant approach for exploring the beginning teaching experience and the teachers themselves, an approach that operates from a restricted conception of teachers and results in relatively predictable conclusions and recommendations. In the process, the important concerns that Susan expressed regarding her ability to make personal sense of her teaching world and to act appropriately within it have generally been neglected. This chapter argues that the special nature of teaching itself and the kind of response it requires of new educators have important implications for any research designed to address the phenomenon of beginning to teach—and for those who wish to support and improve the practice of beginning teachers.

THE NEW TEACHER'S EXPERIENCE PORTRAYED IN PREVIOUS RESEARCH

The knowledge base for examining new teachers and the process of beginning to teach is found in fewer than 100 studies. These efforts have been reviewed, summarized, and interpreted in several recent reports (Applegate et al., 1977; Johnston, 1986–1987; Johnston & Ryan, 1983; Veenman, 1984; Zeichner, 1983). The reviews report a common direction to the inquiry:

> The most frequent type of research literature on beginning teachers in the past five decades has focused in one form or another on the problems of the beginning teacher—a fact precisely parallel in the nonresearch literature. The orientation of this research has varied little in the past 50 years. (Johnston & Ryan, p. 141)

Plagued by Problems

Following this pattern, surveys, interviews, and rating scales have been used to identify, categorize, and prioritize areas of difficulty encountered by new teachers—their problems. As described by the investigators, this work has been designed to provide a basis for improving supervisory support, upgrading preservice and inservice instruction, evaluating teacher education or induction programs, and predicting the performance of beginning teachers in varied settings. Consequently, studies generally followed a common direction of identifying critical problems and providing relevant suggestions for addressing them.

Many of the problems thus specified were procedural or technical in their nature. Their origins were seen to lie in the fact that relevant information and skills from a sound pedagogical knowledge base were not applied efficiently and effectively to the issues at hand. Typical of these were studies such as Barr and Rudisill (1930), Johnson and Umstattd (1932), Kyte (1936), Strickland (1956), Tower (1956), Wallace (1951), and Wey (1951). On most of these lists of problems experienced by new teachers, student discipline ranked highest; motivating students, dealing with individual differences, assessing student work, and relating to parents followed (Veenman, 1984).

Restricted by Ineffective Thinking

Another cluster of research studies focused on the psychosocial difficulties beginning teachers experienced as they began their teaching careers. This line of inquiry advanced the notion that problems were not dealt with effectively by new teachers, because a breakdown occurred in their thinking operations. Beginning professionals were not able to identify relevant elements of problematic situations and apply appropriate treatments, because conditions prevented them from thinking rationally. Both the innerdirected nature of this focus of inquiry and its conclusions increased the seriousness of its implications for new teachers and for those concerned with their development and support. Helping them solve problems was no longer enough; beginners were not even able to perceive and approach dilemmas accurately and reflectively.

For instance, Sarason (1982) argued that the beginning years of teaching might be expected to be difficult and disappointing for young teachers and their schools alike. He felt that incompatible and often conflicting needs, expectations, and access to relevant knowledge on the parts of both new teachers and their schools created situations where problems were all but inevitable. Lortie (1975) examined what he identified as demanding and nonsupportive environments of schools in relation to new teachers. Given these conditions, high stress and anxiety were assumed probable, and "if it is true that too much anxiety retards learning, some beginning teachers will have difficulty making accurate perceptions and thoughtful decisions as they learn the job" (p. 72). Glassberg (1980) also cited the anxiety experienced by beginning teachers because of a demanding and insensitive school environment, "a situation in which it is difficult for the teacher to accurately perceive situations, to make decisions, and to act in a thoughtful and deliberate fashion" (p. 9). She suggested that new teachers were apt to regress in their levels of thinking and to interpret new information in old ways. Corcoran (1981) went further and described the new teachers she studied as "paralyzed," incapable of using the resources they had been provided during their preservice training. Sorenson (1967) reported that student teachers "rarely referred to what they were trying to accomplish with their pupils but only to how, and not at all to the applications of theory except to warn against it" (p. 177).

Effects on Students

Even more serious, another group of studies indicated that the difficulties young teachers encountered in problem-solving and thinking were likely to be reflected in their actions toward students. For example, new teachers and student teachers appeared to use more rigid, punitive measures after they were exposed to the realities of classrooms and schools (Hoy, 1968, 1969; Hoy & Rees, 1977; Iannacone, 1963; Tabachnick, 1980). These reports concluded that, because most school cultures equated good teaching with student control, beginning teachers were socialized into adopting a more punitive and custodial pupil control ideology that came to direct their teaching practice.

ALTERNATIVE VIEWS OF NEW TEACHERS AND THEIR EXPERIENCES

On the other hand, if we return to Susan, who introduced this chapter, paralysis, lack of theory, or even rigidity did not appear to characterize her concern and unrest accurately. Susan, a first-year math teacher in a multi-ethnic, diverse socioeconomic inner-city middle school, had actively been trying to "put things in order" in her new teaching situation. The area she had been concentrating on when her principal intervened was that of organizing student behaviors according to which merited different kinds and intensities of responding. From her comments, an observer could almost see an image in her mind of all possible student offenses being laid out and ordered from very trivial to most serious. Perhaps Susan even pictured herself inserting dividers at certain points along the line to indicate categories for behaviors that should be, for example, ignored, dealt with in the classroom, or reported to the office. It was an orderly, predictable schematic she apparently envisioned as possible and desirable.

But Susan's efforts at order were thwarted by not having all the data with which she needed to work. New pieces of information were added daily that gave old pieces different meanings. Colleagues and administrators with whom she worked attributed different interpretations to what Susan had assumed as givens. Alternative priorities and goals demanded consideration. Susan was pulled by the tensions and contradictions within daily school life as she tried to respond to particular, problematic situations in consistent, principled ways. Making sense of—as well as contributing to—the sense of her world were qualities she prized and strove to bring about, but not ones that were readily accomplished.

Susan's experience, when compared to that portrayed by previous studies of beginning teachers, was notably different. Even though, if faced with a survey in which she was required to identify the nature of her problems from lists of predefined selections Susan might well choose terms such as *discipline* or *dealing with administrators,* it is unlikely that she herself would voluntarily describe her experience in those terms. Susan did not view her difficulties as isolated categories of problems to which she sought routine solutions. Instead, she attempted to construct meanings, to recognize patterns, and to build consistencies in her interpretations and her actions. She engaged in a process of observing her surroundings carefully while grouping instances of similar experiences together. She mentally recorded the comments and responses of people around her to check her perceptions and conclusions. She implemented actions and noted their effects while evaluating her current thinking against her findings. Her conclusions were tentative and perhaps not those reached through formalized study; her actions were experimental and might not have conveyed consistency to an observer. It could well have been in these differences between new teachers' construction of meanings and those conceptions used in traditional literature that ideas of "paralyzed" and "theoryless" beginning teachers were born.

EMERGING RESEARCH ABOUT TEACHERS AND TEACHING

On the other hand, some more recent study of experienced teachers has shifted away from that which previously concentrated primarily on observable teacher behaviors and other variables that were clearly segmentable and amenable to measurement (Shavelson & Stern, 1981). A growing body of literature focuses on exploring and reconstructing the implicit theories that teachers use as conceptual frameworks for their thinking and acting (see, for example, Duffy, 1977; Elbaz, 1983; Janesick, 1977; Munby, 1982). Clark and Peterson (1986) cited nine studies that focus directly on what they identify as teachers' implicit theories of teaching and learning. Considerable variation appears to be found in the focus and substance of these teacher-constructed theories, suggesting that contextual factors apparently contribute significantly to their formation. Some common elements characterize the research studies as a group:

1. Inquiry is approached through small sample descriptive research,

drawing on methods of inquiry that include ethnographic field study, clinical interviews, stimulated recall, and the repertory grid technique.

2. The labels describing the focus of study vary (e.g., teachers' personal perspectives, conceptual systems, practical knowledge, and implicit theories) and each term has a somewhat different meaning. However, "they hold in common the idea that a teacher's cognitive and other behaviors are guided by and make sense in relation to a personally-held system of beliefs, values and principles" (Clark & Peterson, 1986, p. 287).

3. The researchers view their central task as constructing an explicit description of teachers' implicitly-held theories in ways that do not violate teachers' personal conceptions of what they believe and act on.

A SHIFT IN PERSPECTIVE TOWARD TEACHERS THEMSELVES

Focus on teachers' theories is grounded in an effort to raise the understanding of the practice of teaching from a primarily technical perspective that concentrates on isolated processes such as those problem areas found in much of the beginning teacher research. The theory-oriented perspective attempts to construct a more adequate portrayal of the complex, interactive, and reflective operations that are involved in teachers' daily judgments about teaching dilemmas. Operating under the assumption that teachers themselves (like others) are only able to articulate partially the theories by which they interpret and act in their teaching worlds, the researcher works to identify and reconstruct these frames of reference, usually through systematic analysis of interview and observation data. Through this process, efforts are made to open teacher-held norms and assumptions for examination, expose consistencies and inconsistencies within and between thought and action, and evaluate orientations for their practical and moral efficacy.

It is important to emphasize that interest in exploring the implicit theories of teachers reflects more than movement toward a different focus of study or a shift in research methodology alone. A particular world view or paradigm directed studies in which teacher problems were identified or behaviors observed and recorded to substantiate or refute formal abstract theory. A substantially different perspective guides contemporary inquiry, which seeks to understand a theoretical orientation within the words and actions of practitioners in schools. The contrast between these diverse approaches involves different perceptions of such basic notions as knowledge, knowing, and theory itself—and, subsequently, about the ways teachers themselves are conceived.

A Hierarchy Within Conceptions of Theory

Many traditional studies of teachers in general and new teachers in particular assumed that "real" theory could only be found in particular circumstances and could only be created by certain people operating in specialized conditions. A dichotomy was set up between theory found in what was labeled the "theoretical mode" and that called the "practical" (see, for example, Gauthier, 1963; Schwab, 1969, for discussion of the theoretical/practical distinction). The practical specified an approach for arriving at a decision that could be used to guide possible action in a particular situation. On the other hand, "real" theory was equated with that which was abstract, universal, and timeless. Accordingly, theory in the theoretical mode—which met these criteria—was considered "better," of more worth, than that found in practical usage.

Although not often acknowledged, this hierarchy within orientations toward theory is often found in educational literature. Lortie (1975), for example, proposed that teachers did not have a technical culture, a set of empirically-tested practices and pedagogical principles that were accepted by the profession. Lacking these universals, teachers needed to resort to personally-designed practices derived from experience and conversation. In an earlier, influential work, Jackson (1968) observed that teachers were "conceptually simple;" the specificity of the teaching situations with which they had to deal impeded the development and use of "true" theory. Huberman (1983) attributed teachers' reliance on intuition and impulse, rather than on reason, as a necessary consequence of having to respond continually to immediate classroom demands.

The theory that the experienced teachers in this literature "lacked" was a form that is viewed as existing apart from and actually transcending experience and action—particularly as these elements are encountered in particular instances. This position regarding theory arises from the Positivist orientation to the Social Sciences, that is, a perspective that assumes that principles of knowing in areas addressed by the Social Sciences are the same as those treated in the Natural Sciences (see, for example, Comte, 1975; Descartes, 1969; Durkheim, 1982; Mill, 1959). Because mastery and use of universal laws are considered necessary for predicting and ultimately controlling the social as well as the physical environment (regarded as the ultimate goals of thought and action), when teachers do not reflect "proper" application of these formalized laws in their pure forms, the educators' conceptual functioning, as well as the effectiveness of their actions, may be—and often have been—questioned. Beginning teachers appear to be particularly deficient when these criteria are applied.

Qualities of Practical Theorizing

Given the prevalence of this older tradition of teacher research, study of teachers' implicit theories represents a qualitatively different perspective to what is considered knowing and theorizing; in turn, this different perspective has significant implications for conceptions of preservice and inservice teacher education. Rather than theory being conceived as a complete, acontextual, universal entity that is created elsewhere and applied to a particular problem or situation for resolution, theory making is viewed as being an ongoing process, a conversation of active, thoughtful individuals—like teachers—with their environments as they test the abstract against the concrete, the general against the specific, the whole against its parts. Theory is conceived as reflective, dialectic, dynamic, and evolving. Schön (1983) sketched a picture of this interplay as he illustrated the way skilled practitioners in other fields engaged in an ongoing cycle of observing, hypothesizing, testing, and reflecting.

Two other qualities of "practical" theorizing are important to note in determining how this orientation is different from formal theory in form and use. First, practical theory is viewed as contextual in that it occurs in and considers seriously the continually developing interplay of a special combination of historical, social, economic, and political forces. As Bolan (1980) observed, the practical theorist must consider the world as a whole and cannot enjoy the luxury of isolating particular elements for attention. From this perspective, problems do not divide neatly and must be dealt with in the particular contexts—including competing dilemmas—in which they are found.

Second, practical theorizing presumes and becomes an integral component of action. Consideration of alternatives, consequences, and goals must be made bearing in mind the risks and commitments necessary when acting in situations where a variety of different needs and interests are at stake. Consistent with the thinking of Arendt (1958), true action cannot be capricious, habitual, or reflexive; rather, the kind of action and thus theorizing that is conceived is undertaken in conjunction with serious, informed, and reflective thought.

Implications of Conceptions of Theory for Teachers and Teaching

In brief, research directed toward teachers' theories presumes a complex and changing world of practice from which theory arises and on which it is based. In taking this position, implicit theory research also assumes and reinforces a particular conception of teachers—active rather than passive, professionals instead of technicians, reflective rather than merely receptive. From this perspective, teachers cannot only apply objective facts and principles to particular situations. They must consider any action against what its likely consequences might be for serving important human needs and satisfying important human purposes (Sockett, 1987; Tom, 1984; Zeichner & Liston, 1987). Educators need to be able to see beyond what presently exists to envision what could be better in terms of such issues as fairness and justice. These conditions imply that teachers often need to be creators rather than solely consumers of knowledge and theory.

Orientations that gave rise to interest in the implicit theories of teachers were based on qualitatively different conceptions of teachers than those held by much earlier study. Not only does this different view of teachers reflect in the focus and approach for research but, equally significant, it directs the implications and recommendations for policy and practice that emanate from the inquiry. For example, the practice of teaching may be conceived primarily as a rule-governed activity in which facts, principles, and procedures from a body or professional knowledge are "applied" to problem situations to bring about designated goals. If new teachers are not observed to engage in the application process effectively, they may be described as stupefied, because the use of abstract theory has been equated with good thinking. Furthermore, if this good thinking is only considered possible in situations devoid of emotion and stress, the controlled conditions of research laboratories will always offer distinct advantages over the classrooms of beginning teachers.

When measured against these specialized criteria, it is not surprising that new teachers do not excel. More seriously, in the research process, impressions are created about the beginners' functioning and potential that then serve as the bases of recommendations for induction policies and practices. This situation is potentially more consequential at the present time when greater attention is being focused on entry into the teaching profession and supportive and instructional induction programs are being developed and, at times, mandated. It is troublesome to consider that the structures and approaches proposed may well operate to bring about and reinforce the very pessimistic views of beginning teachers in which the studies were originally framed.

Concern about the theoretical orientations dominating most previous beginning teacher research and the conclusions and recommendations arising from it led to the study of first-year teachers in which Susan was a part. A study design was developed that built on the experience of research on the implicit theories of teachers and allowed the exploration of whether and how new teachers constructed meanings for their thinking and acting. New teachers were approached as potentially-reflective persons, and efforts were made to examine and reconstruct the implicit theories they used as conceptual organizers for their teaching practice. One area of their theory-making activity is described briefly in the account that follows; it is reflective of other areas that were studied and developed in the larger project of which this was a part (Copa & Swanson, 1984).

A STUDY OF BEGINNING TEACHERS

Five new teachers were followed throughout their first year of teaching. The group had been selected to include a diversity in subject areas taught: Agriculture, English, Home Economics, Mathematics, and Science. In addition, the teaching sites of the three men and two women represented urban, suburban, and rural settings, parochial and public schools, and junior and senior high school levels.

The teachers were visited four times during the school year, and four consecutive school days were spent with each during these times. The first visits were arranged to permit seeing the new teachers as early in the school year as possible, and three other sessions followed spaced approximately two months apart.

During the visits, a number of different kinds of interviews, some formally structured and others less formally organized, were conducted as the primary means of assessing the *thought* of the teachers. Ethnoscience interviews probed the categories and relationships used by teachers to structure their perceptions of their classrooms and act on them. Life-history interviews were designed to gain understanding of how early experiences—both family and school—influenced the beliefs and practices of the teachers. Semi-structured and unstructured interviews proved most valuable for examining the occurrences that took place in the classroom and the explanations the teachers had for their own actions. The interviews were recorded on tape and transcribed before being analyzed.

The *actions* of the teachers were examined through systematic observations inside and outside their classrooms and by more limited examination of student worksheets and written assignments. Observations included some that involved mapping and calendar study, census taking, and kinesics (Birdwhistell, 1970; Dobbert, 1982; Spradley, 1980). However, most of the observing time was directed toward timed observations in which dialogue, facial and body expressions, and contextual factors involved in classroom interactions were carefully recorded in detail.

Ethnographic analysis techniques were used to examine and analyze the data. Recorded interviews and observations were studied for the presence of recurring themes. Concepts and their relationships were organized into hierarchies and taxonomies based on how and where words and actions were used in several different contexts. Particular attention was given to identifying and reconstructing the meanings teachers held for elements within their teaching experience. The availability of observational as well as interview data provided a rich opportunity for testing preliminary notions against both the thoughts and actions of the teachers. Gradually, it was possible to construct the patterns that underlay the teachers' theories behind particular thoughts and actions.

ENERGY IN NEW TEACHERS' THOUGHTS

The study had been planned originally to examine the theories teachers used to think about students and to make judgments about appropriate actions concerning them. This goal was accomplished; however, in the process, a strong, pervasive theme emerged that ultimately appeared to provide better understanding of many other areas of the teachers' theory-making activities. This theme was identified by the label used most commonly by teachers, *energy,* and is presented in this chapter as an illustration of the theory-making efforts of new teachers.

During the third round of visits to the teachers in the study, I noted that many of them used the word *energy* when describing their thoughts about certain situations and when explaining the reasons behind their actions. Continual reference to this phenomenon provoked me to return to interview transcripts and field notes to examine when and how teachers used the word, hopefully determining if the idea it represented was used by the teachers as a construct for organizing their experiences. It was not until the end of the fourth and final round of visits that I first used the label "energy" with the teachers and tested their reactions to the tentative relationships I thought were found in what they had said and/or done previously.

When early interviews (from first and second visits) were examined, it appeared that energy represented a real and quantifiable entity to these young teachers. They seemed to regard it as a resource or commodity and, as such, assigned to it many of the attributes of other finite resources such as time and money:

> You've only got so much energy in you to give. . . . I have just so much emotional energy that I can give out; as a result, I have to decide who is in greatest need of that. . . . (C,4)[1]

> I think of myself today as having a certain amount of energy each day to relate to teaching. (E,4)

---

[1] The codes following quotations from the teachers denote the particular teachers—for example, teacher "C"—and the number of the visit—for example, visit 4.

It's because I'm not trying to do so many things at once. I can focus more energy on what I am doing. (B,3)

I don't have to use so much energy on those classes. (C,3)

Furthermore, the teachers consciously appeared to employ this substance, "energy," to bring about desired results in their classrooms. They attempted to manipulate its use and control its flow:

It takes a lot of energy, but it really solves a lot of discipline problems if I really emphasize the work with Jimmy Olson. (E,4)

This way, I know it's at the end. I know if I can weather this out, I can burn my energy if I have to to keep this class down and, if I come up a little limp, so what? It's the end. I've made it. (C,4)

Oh, yeah. He drives me nuts. Sometimes I get really ticked at him. I don't want to deal with him. He takes eight times more energy. Frankly, I'd rather put the energy in on Adam who is going to listen. (E,4)

DISTINGUISHING THE NATURE OF ENERGY

As the importance of the energy concept to the teachers became apparent, I reviewed previous transcripts of interviews and questioned teachers more specifically about their views. From this information, it was possible to construct a rather detailed picture of how the teachers perceived being "high" or "low" in energy in terms of the synonyms, metaphors, feelings, and action tendencies (e.g., "everything falls into place and you go, 'whew' ") they used. Figure 1 summarizes the words and phrases teachers used to portray their notions of energy. Their verbal descriptors were marked by indications of direction, motion, and technological analogies. Teachers also reflected on the relationship of physical and psychological energy, with one person summarizing what others had said in different words: "Mental stress can kill you or physical stress will—or at least wreck your life. Physical, I guess, can have a more permanent and devastating effect on you; but mental— I think will get you first" (C,4).

In addition to discussing the meanings of energy, teachers described the factors that tended to increase their energy level and those that operated to decrease it (see Figure 2). When these factors were plotted by their sources, it was quite evident that, whereas almost all the factors that decreased a teacher's energy supply were directly school related, more than half of those that contributed positively to the supply came from out-of-school sources. This phenomenon became important later

HIGH ON ENERGY

IT'S ABOUT THE SAME AS BEING:

MOTIVATED	EXCITED
UP	RE-EXCITED
ENTHUSED	HYPED-UP
ALERT	PSYCHED-UP

I TEND TO ACT LIKE I:

HAVE HIGH EXPECTATIONS	AM SATISFIED
AM FULL OF IDEAS	AM LOOKING FOR NEW THINGS TO DO
AM NOT FALLING ASLEEP	CAN PUT IN A LOT OF EFFORT
HAVE RENEWED INTEREST	AM GOING BEYOND WHAT'S NECESSARY
CAN FUNCTION BETTER	EVERYTHING FALLS INTO PLACE AND YOU GO "WHEW"

IT MAKES ME FEEL:

POSITIVE	EXCITED
PRETTY GOOD	LIKE I'M NOT JUST SURVIVING
STRONGER	
GOOD	LIKE NOTHING CAN GO WRONG
BETTER	

IT'S LIKE BEING:

PUMPED-UP	FIRED-UP
WOUND-UP	ON THE TOP LOOKING DOWN
CRANKING	
WIRED	MARATHON MAN
IN HIGH GEAR	ON A RUSH
ON TRACK	ABLE TO CUT LOOSE
ABLE TO START THE DAY OVER AGAIN	INTO THE SWING OF THINGS

LOW ON ENERGY

I TEND TO ACT LIKE I:

DON'T EXPECT TO ENJOY THE DAY	NEED TO REMOVE MYSELF
WANT TO REST OR SLEEP	MUST AVOID THINKING ABOUT SCHOOL
SEE NO HOPE FOR SATISFACTION	JUST GET BY WITH WHAT HAS TO BE DONE
DON'T WANT TO DO ANYTHING	COULDN'T HAVE CARED LESS
AM SLOWLY DRIFTING	
DREAD COMING TO WORK	LOST A LOT OF INTEREST

IT'S ABOUT THE SAME AS BEING:

FRUSTRATED	OVERWHELMED
DEPRESSED	LAZY
EXHAUSTED	FRAZZLED
NOT ENTHUSED ENOUGH	NOT UP

IT MAKES ME FEEL:

SO TIRED	INADEQUATE
EXHAUSTED	DOWN—IN A BAD MOOD
PERSONALLY AND EMOTIONALLY LOW	PHYSICALLY TIRED
BAD	I'M BACK TO SURVIVAL

IT'S LIKE BEING:

DRAINED	BURNED OUT
IN A RUT	DOWN
DRAGGED DOWN	SET BACK
IN LOW GEAR	BOGGED DOWN
GRASPING AT THE RIM TRYING TO KEEP FROM DROWNING	
LIKE I'VE JUST BEEN THROUGH THE WAR	

FIGURE 1. Defining the Nature of Energy.

in the study when efforts were made to understand teachers' actions in relation to these interpretations.

During my third round of visits during February and early March, a substantial shift was evident in what was observed in classrooms and in what was being said in interviews. Before that time, only one teacher had verbally set limits to what he was willing to do to carry out his teaching responsibilities. During the late winter months, the use of the word "energy" was heard more often, and other teachers expressed the view that they were no longer able or willing to expend the unlimited amount of effort they had been investing in teaching. The following was but one of several statements that illustrated the feelings eventually voiced by all the teachers:

It started after Christmas. I just decided that I needed to spend some

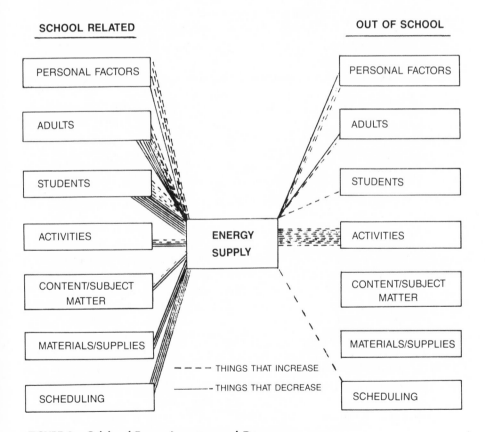

FIGURE 2. Origin of Energy Increasers and Decreasers.

more time just sitting and relaxing. I wanted to do not a whole lot of social things that you can do up here—I enjoy doing them though—but just personal things: keeping my apartment in just a little better shape and I needed to just spend more time shopping. . . . So, I just needed to do some more types of things for myself with outside-of-school activities and so that was sort of a resolution on my own part just to take less time with it and if it didn't exactly pull off the way I'd hoped it would, tough! (B,3)

These statements were considered particularly significant, because they appeared to signal the pivotal point at which teachers felt they had constructed sufficient sense of one important element of their worlds that they could attempt to manipulate conditions related to this area to bring about their own ends. At this time in the year, they expressed the belief that it was necessary to maintain a certain balance of what they called "energy," and that they themselves could affect the maintenance of that balance. The sense making that the teachers had developed in their thoughts was ready to be translated into action.

By studying the patterns of their actions displayed in observations and examining these actions in reference to the teachers' own interpretations, it was possible to organize a schema that represented how teachers purposively acted on the information and beliefs they had systematically developed about energy (see Figure 3). Case illustrations were developed to represent how the components of the figure were found in the particular contexts in which each teacher worked; all cases are found in the longer report.

ENERGY IN TEACHERS' ACTIONS

A brief example from one of these case studies illustrates in part the relatively systematic and reflective manner in which teachers went about testing and reforming their thought and action in relation to one another. The example is drawn from "Adapt Curriculum and Learning Experiences," one of the areas in which teachers appeared to try to maintain a balance of energy within important classroom activities (number 4 in Figure 3).

In the observation, "The Rise and Fall of Math Enrichment Days," found in the study report (Copa & Swanson, 1984), Susan implements a lesson she has planned for several days. It is early fall, and she presents the day to her students as a reward for good work. She makes provisions for calculators, a film, and high student involvement activities. A film projector is secured, and students are asked to bring calculators from home to supplement the limited school supply. From

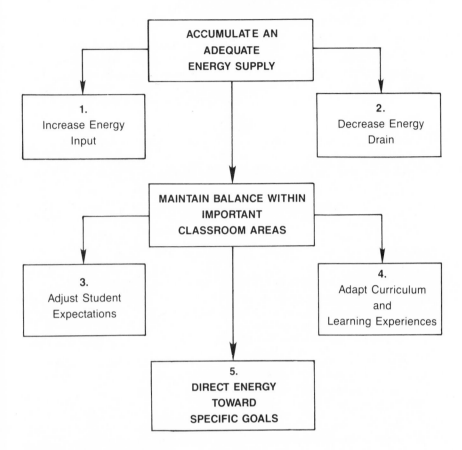

FIGURE 3.   Energy in Action.

a particularly rowdy arrival of students to a difficult-to-manage distribution of very few calculators (no one brought any from home) through loud and disruptive latecomers, the end of third period finds Susan recording "warnings" on a piece of paper on her desk while shouting, "I'm not going to wait any longer! If you don't be quiet, we're going to table this!"

When I returned in early December and later in February, there were no days designated particularly as Math Enrichment Days. I attempted to inquire about their fate in a nonthreatening way, but Susan was not hesitant about discussing what had happened:

It's just been the whole time and energy thing and that (the special days) helped, especially for my eighth grade. It's just getting bogged down and not having time for anything but what you see as the essentials; you know, recording the grades, keeping kids after school and that's kind of too bad.

It was just sort of like energy on days when I just felt so bad. . . . Oh, I had some calculators taken too and I felt like, "Oh, shoot!" It just took the steam out of. . . . And, I showed another movie that they were just real antsy. . . .

The other thing is just, I guess not being that familiar with the material. So, it takes so long just to present the material in a clear way that I don't really have that many ideas about interesting things to do with it yet. (E,4)

Susan continued to find ways to integrate manipulative activities into her classes, but she often pondered whether the energy she expended in preparing and carrying out these experiences would be better spent in other ways. The activity classes were difficult to handle, and distributing and retrieving materials was demanding. She seemed to decide that she needed to establish better control over the "essentials" before she tackled what she labeled "the frosting on the cake." Some of the advice she said she would give new teachers was:

Just do what you have to do to survive; just organize things so it's easy on yourself, because you're going to have so many things coming at you so fast. And, just give yourself a lot of leeway, a lot of room to make mistakes and stuff. (E,4)

I talked with Susan the following year. She was still at the same school, but she reported that a number of factors had made the year much more pleasant and her classrooms more manageable. She said she had been able to do many more creative activities with her students, and she felt much better about teaching.

THE ROLE OF ENERGY IN NEW TEACHERS' EXPERIENCES

Energy in a Stage Theory of Concerns

There are different ways to think about the reflections of these new teachers concerning energy and specifically about how Susan used the idea to understand and act in relation to her math class. Readers who are familiar with the beginning teacher literature will doubtlessly see reflections of what Fuller (1969) described as the "survival" stage within a teacher's career. According to Fuller, after a preservice period characterized by idealism and a tendency to identify with the student role, concerns of new teachers changed drastically when they were first confronted with being a real teacher in a real school. They then concentrated on their own survival as teachers as they focused on classroom control, their own mastery of the content to be taught, and evaluations by their supervisors. Similar to Maslow's (1970, 1971) elemental condition of safety, it has been assumed that beginning teachers require a secure foundation in certain basic conditions before they are able to "move forward"; for example, in Fuller's hierarchy to become concerned about, first, the quality of their instruction and later about the well-being of their students. If this interpretation is accepted, energy might be viewed as a version of or a component within the concern for survival. Certainly, the value held by teachers in this study for maintenance of a prescribed amount of whatever the energy construct represented seems to indicate attention to aspects of survival.

On the other hand, the idea of a stage model and energy's role as a foundational element in a hierarchy weaken when tested by other observations. When it was possible to be with teachers periodically over the span of their entire first year of teaching while interviewing them extensively, a "stage" structure became questionable. In this study, teachers were not observed to move in a sequential and systematic manner from a lower level set of concerns to those identified by Fuller (1975) as being more advanced. Instead, they appeared to move into and out of particular concerns depending on contextual factors that influenced and were influenced by the teachers' personal sense of well-being. "Energy" played an interesting role in how they explained this process.

I introduced the idea of a hierarchical system of concerns to Susan in order to test if she found the model useful for understanding her experiences. After briefly describing Fuller's (1975) stages, I asked for her reaction. Susan thought for a time and replied that she definitely could recognize elements of the stages in the issues she found troublesome; however, she had difficulty viewing them as occurring in a sequential order:

like this circular model—even the one you first said: first survival, then it's this, then it's that. I think it's so hard to tell.

I feel like I go back and forth on that and it really does relate to the amount of energy I have—or just when I don't have a lot of energy. [Then] I'm just like maybe I'm just back to survival. I might have a survival week or two and then, for lots of different reasons, things go better and I have a little more energy to think about the students and what really would be best for them and that kind of thinking. (E,4)

Thus, energy might be thought of by the teachers as a mechanism employed to move them back and forth between and among kinds and levels of concerns. On the other hand, if one watched the new teachers for any length of time and participated in their daily lives, it became quite evident that they did not have the luxury of dealing with concerns in an hierarchical order or according to any schema that separated concerns into categories or otherwise removed them from other considerations. The situations that the teachers dealt with daily did not come categorized as survival, instructional, and/or student concerns. Rather, each situation generally embodied multiple concerns and issues and interests, all of which demanded attention and consideration simultaneously and precluded the selection of a solution based solely on one or the other. This is exactly the situation Susan was describing at the beginning of this chapter as she agonized over the problems of consistency and certainty.

Energy Found in the Tensions of Teaching
Because of this situation, rather than a linear, hierarchical model for describing the beginning teaching experience and the role a construct such as energy might play in it, it appears that more potential may be found in the idea of tension and uncertainty. Recently, an increasing amount of literature has focused on the uncertain or undefined nature of the issues and problems with which professionals such as teachers need to deal (Berlak & Berlak, 1981; Floden & Clark, 1987; Jackson, 1986; Lampert, 1984, 1985; Schön, 1983, 1987; Zeichner & Liston, 1987). Particularly useful is a description of the characteristics of unclear problems suggested by Reid (1979). According to his explanation, problems of this nature:

• require that judgments about action be made,
• involve issues and factors that are changing and uncertain,
• rest in specific social and historical settings,
• are unique in the particular combination of people, events, and circumstances that need to be considered,
• necessitate the weighing and evaluating of competing values and goals,
• are unpredictable in terms of projecting exactly what will happen if alternative actions were taken, and
• demand that they be considered carefully, because there is reason to believe that what is decided can lead to better states of affairs for all involved.

These were the types of situations that Susan and the other teachers confronted. Armed with the general principles and information from their preservice education and lengthy experience with schools, they likely set out to "solve" problems as they pictured good professionals should. However, they discovered that each situation was unique in special kinds of ways and insidiously evaded routine treatments. For instance, one had to consider Chris' learning difficulties, that Pat had been moved recently to a group home because of incest, and Mr. Sullivan's personality quirks. It was important to remember that the children came from one of two grossly different socioeconomic groups, that the sixth grade class had had five teachers the previous year, and that Jerry's father beat him if he thought his son was messing up at school. It certainly was significant that the children learned math, but it was also important that they began to see school and teachers as pleasant contacts and themselves as capable people. In the process, it was necessary for a teacher to have rest and some life of his or her own. Meanwhile, it was hard to tell how Lisa would react if she were kept after school or if the detention would actually provoke more completed homework. It seemed to work well last week when a surprise quiz was given or George's mother was called or the students worked in small groups, but would it this week?

A multitude of questions arose. A score of competing issues and considerations presented themselves. All pulled in different directions and demanded attention. The countless uncertainties, most likely unanticipated and unprepared for, would be challenging enough by themselves for anyone; however, teachers could not only marvel at the confusion; they needed to act and to act wisely.

What then about energy? The foregoing conception of the experience of teaching suggests an alternative interpretation to its being part of a stage theory of concerns. If one pictured the circumstances encountered by new teachers as episodes containing contradictory forces, opposing values and considerations in tension, multiple realities and relevant factors operating simultaneously, then the teachers may have developed a theory of energy to attempt to understand, to create order and balance, to reduce—if not resolve—the uncertainties and resultant tensions, and to establish a basis for acting reasonably in what otherwise was an unreasonable situation. In other words, the theories of new teachers (illustrated here in the description of energy) may have served to give meaning and relationship to what otherwise would have remained isolated, "unique" episodes.

Susan's experience with Math Enrichment Days offers an opportunity to examine how this way of thinking may have come about. Susan originally described the day of special high-involvement activities as a time for students to enjoy math-related experiences. She also wanted to "try out" teaching approaches she had seen or heard being used successfully that did not fit into the text-driven curriculum she generally followed. As the day approached, she used its promise as an incentive for conscientious student work and threat of its removal as punishment for bad behavior. When the event actually arrived, Susan appeared to expect students to be "on task," in their seats, and "reasonably" quiet. Math Enrichment Days had achieved Reid's criterion of necessitating the *weighing and evaluating of competing values and goals.*

Susan had assumed some conditions that never came to be and had not anticipated others that actually did. She asked her students days ahead to bring pocket calculators, but they did not; on subsequent enrichment days, school calculators actually disappeared. It appeared impossible for some students to work together with anyone else, and they employed loud disruptions to alleviate their discomfort. Indications of jealousy, competition, and power permeated the calculator distribution process. Years of traditions, procedures, and policies; ideas about school and roles and learning; unique personalities and needs and social groupings; expectations by teacher and students and administrators—all created a *context that was unique, dynamic, and unpredictable.*

Films generally "bombed" in this class of TV addicts. Distributing calculators to classes of almost 30 students defied all efforts for system and order. Group work often disintegrated into bedlam and deafening noise. It was hard to predict and control the results of various approaches. It was even more difficult to regroup and implement counterstrategies when the unexpected actually occurred. Thus, *means or strategies and their consequences were difficult to calculate and to implement.*

Susan went back and reflected on the dilemmas involving goals and contexts and means, what she had learned, and what it meant for what she did next. She, like the other teachers studied, found sense in what she thought about energy. For example, it took a great deal of her "energy" to prepare for and implement Math Enrichment Days; on the other hand, an undesirable amount of undirected "energy" was produced by students. Because energy balance was considered desirable and imbalance was becoming more intense, measures needed to be taken to bring conditions back into line. In the process, certain goals were put aside or postponed in favor of others, some contextual factors were acknowledged and worked around or with (whereas attempts were made to influence others), and alternative strategies were weighed and reevaluated for their projected and actual outcomes. Theories of energy seemed to work well to reconcile or reduce the contradictions or tensions between some elements of the situation. They may also have masked or created illusions when others were considered.

Eisner's (1984) observations about the strengths and limitations of theory are particularly relevant when the experientially-derived theories of these new teachers are considered:

> Like language, theory is both an asset and a liability. It is an asset because it provides guidelines for perception; it points us in directions that enable us to see. But it is also a liability because, while it provides the windows through which we obtain focus, it creates walls that hamper our perception of those qualities and processes that are not addressed by the concepts we have chosen to use. Our theoretical frameworks function as templates for perception—every template conceals some parts of the landscape just as it brings other parts to our attention. (p. 450)

Likewise, the theories of the new teachers in the energy study blocked views of certain areas within their experience while increasing the clarity of others. Because of this process, theories such as those that centered on energy have implications for those who work with aspiring and beginning teachers and who study their development.

MESSAGES FOR SUPERVISORS AND TEACHER EDUCATORS

Floden and Clark (1987), in highlighting the indefinite nature of teaching, emphasized the importance of "Preparing Teachers for Uncertainty." There are no doubt many ways one might approach this task, but I suggest that one of the most reasonable is to help new teachers consider more effectively the tensions they are likely to encounter in the contexts, goals, and means of their teaching worlds. This process likely involves recognizing and employing a broader range of knowledge and ways of thinking about teaching than have been considered in the past.

Context and the Beginning Teacher

As discussed at the beginning of this chapter, traditional approaches to thinking about teaching as a science and the subsequent preparation and inservice instruction of teachers minimize, if not ignore, the role of contextual factors in an educator's experience. Like laboratory scientists, teachers are supposed to focus on relevant aspects of issues (while evidently controlling for "extraneous" variables?) and apply appropriate pedagogical principles or laws. When the new teachers in the study described in this chapter found a scientific model to be untenable in actual practice, and as they responded to a natural tendency to create meaning and order in their worlds, theories like energy were developed. The energy theories of these new teachers differed in important ways from the traditional scientific theories of educational scholars in respect to contextual considerations.

Significantly, the new teachers' theories about energy rose out of the particular contexts of which the teachers were a part and allowed them to acknowledge and respond to these settings. Not unexpectedly, their personal contexts and, consequently, the focus and form of the energy constructs, concentrated heavily on teacher-centered elements: personal feelings, frustrations, aspirations, physical and social needs, misgivings, and commitments. Thus, the energy theories provided a framework that had meaning for the teachers and that addressed their special needs and concerns. Although probably not being able to articulate the process, they apparently had attempted to transform the basis on which they understood and acted on their worlds from the traditional theoretical perspective described earlier, one grounded in a scientific or empirical-analytic perspective, to one evolved from human experience—in this case, their own. In admittedly a limited degree, the effort may have represented the kind and focus of theory conceived by such interpretive social sciences as phenomenology, hermeneutics, and ethnomethodology. On the other hand, these young teachers could only move in this direction through an intuitive, trial-and-error manner, because their background and preparation had not opened them to the possibility of alternative perspectives—particularly to those that permitted a more adequate conception of the contextual elements within their situations. Van Manen (1977) discussed alternative orientations to a technical, instrumental approach for considering unclear or "practical" concerns of teaching. He particularly emphasized the constraints of not being able to make conscious choices between and among clearly recognized and understood perspectives:

> It is not enough simply to make use of an orientation. One must understand the experience of having an orientation and of having a specific one. The teacher must also know how an orientation is being used. (p. 213)

Finding themselves in situations in which familiar models did not serve them well, while not being able to draw from legitimate alternatives, the teachers in this study created theories on which they made judgments about the unclear problems they faced. Of necessity, however, these personally-constructed theories were limited, as they were developed almost entirely from individual experiences and considered only that which the young teachers knew, not that which might tap the possible or optimal. Bourdieu (1971) described succinctly the limiting condition that is created: "The individual who attains an immediate, concrete understanding of the familiar world, of the native atmosphere in which and for which he has been brought up, is thereby deprived of the possibility of appropriating immediately and fully the world that lies outside" (p. 205).

Buchmann and Schwille (1983) also raised concern about relying on metaphors or theories derived solely from personal experience to the development of new teachers. They suggested that what beginning teachers find to "work" or succeed often comes to determine their overall conception of teaching, even though these approaches may actually hamper their growth as teachers.

> But the rewards of survival are self-evident and reinforce associated behaviors, derived from firsthand experience to begin with. The relative isolation of teachers throughout their career makes cognitive and behavioral traps associated with firsthand experience particularly effective, often beyond the point of diminishing returns. (p. 38)

A particularly critical area of context about which much has been written is especially likely to be minimized or ignored in individually-formulated theory. The social and political structures of teaching and schools, those implicit and explicit reflections of culturally-accepted norms, traditions, and values, may become so ingrained into systems and practices that their origins and functions are never recognized or questioned. In the process, certain unexamined—and undesirable—consequences may result for particular individuals and groups—for example, pupils, new teachers, and/or families.

The relevance of these contextual factors is highlighted in the vastly different situations in which the new teachers in the energy study were found. For example, one of the teachers taught advanced science classes in a school serving a community of upwardly mobile professional families who sent their children to highly regarded colleges and universities after high school graduation. Another taught agriculture in a rural school in which many of his students remained in town or on family farms following graduation. As an observer, I was impressed by the extreme differences in the experiences of these two teachers regarding areas such as, for example, amount and kind of supervision, the extent of parental involvement and expectation, the nature and interests of the students, external control of the curriculum, location of the classrooms in the school building, and so forth. It is revealing that the science teacher was asked by his principal to resign in the middle of the school year after numerous spontaneous visits to this open classroom, comments from teaching colleagues, and complaints from parents. Meanwhile, the agriculture teacher had been observed but once by his principal—in a formal, announced evaluative visit; on days that this teacher was less than prepared for lessons, he closed the door of his self-contained classroom and "winged it" (his words).

This is a very simplified and limited view of some differences in the contextual elements of the two situations; however it may serve to illustrate that, in order to understand what happens in classrooms and why, it is not only necessary to understand the culture of a particular classroom and a school. Educational contexts must also be related to the surrounding social, economic, and political environments and to the events and people that led them to the point at which they were presently found. If new teachers are to operate wisely in all facets of their professional worlds, they need to be alerted to the importance of attending to contextual concerns and be assisted in developing the tools to do this well. Useful perspectives and tools are likely to come from the social sciences such as particular approaches to anthropology, phenomenology, sociology, and communications. These fields of study may open the possibility of systematically examining meanings, values, assumptions, and beliefs that are held and promoted by people in their language, culture, traditions, institutions, and policies. They offer theories that address the kinds of contextual tensions encountered by new teachers while transcending the limitations of individual experience.

Values and Goals in the New Teacher's World

Competing values and goals comprise another area of uncertainty for which new teachers are generally not prepared to deal. Lacking the frameworks and tools for considering normative issues, the teachers in the energy study used their personally constructed theories of energy to resolve dilemmas that involved incompatible values and goals. The origins and structures of these personally created theories often made them less than optimal for addressing the moral elements involved in this area of unclear problems.

Tom (1984) argued that teaching is a distinctly moral activity for two primary reasons: (a) A moral relationship exists between the teacher and student that is unique in the dominant role the teacher plays in respect to power, and (b) a particular curricular plan involves selecting certain objectives or areas of content over others and thus either openly or implicitly implies a valued end. At various times, the teachers in the energy study pondered problem situations in terms of right and wrong actions and in relation to their responsibilities as teachers. For example, Susan was shown to debate about the most justifiable teaching approach to use with her students; other teachers deliberated this issue in respect to laboratory experiences, individual projects, and creative versus more prescriptive assignments. Teachers described quandaries over student behavior, where to "draw the line," and appropriate sanctions to administer for undesirable activities. They openly discussed the issues involved in how much power to share with and to relinquish to students. What is of particular interest, however, and perhaps what should be especially disturbing, is the frequency with which these puzzles were resolved citing energy-related references; the following comments of two of the teachers are typical of the reasoning that was employed in this area:

> Grammar is important. They have to know it. It also fills up time. What would there be if we didn't have it? I'd have another writing session or a short story class. And, I'm not going to assign another writing assignment. [The exhausted English teacher pointed to the pile of ungraded papers on his desk.] (C,3)

> I sat there and watched and that Dickerson would cheat right in front of me; he'd look right at me and do it and that's what he was doing. . . . He'd look at me and ask her and I'd be staring at him. So, finally, I said, "Brenda, do you want to move?"

> She's the one I knew would get a good grade and she's the one they all copy, so I thought I would move her. Trying to get Dickerson to move would probably be like pulling teeth. (A,3)

Thus, what teachers described in theory as meriting moral consideration was frequently acted on using other criteria. One consequence of this situation was that certain critical questions were never asked and some issues appeared not to be considered. Similar to concerns about contextual factors, it is not certain whether these new teachers recognized questions of goals and values as being substantively different from technical, "how-to" quandaries. If they did, it is questionable whether they had the knowledge and skills to deal with them in the systematic, deliberate manner that these special matters required. Contrary to technical questions or even contextual concerns, consideration of issues involving values and goals requires means for looking beyond what presently exists to determine what might be and weigh what should. In this process, "the central questions ask which educational goals, experiences, and activities lead toward forms of life which are mediated by concerns for justice, equity, and concrete fulfillment, and whether current arrangements serve important human needs and satisfy important human purposes" (Zeichner & Liston, 1987, p. 25).

Seriously considering competing values and goals involves particular orientations or dispositions: a sincere belief that what teachers do or do not do can lead to better conditions for those involved (Reid, 1979), acknowledgment of teaching as a socially constructed phenomenon that may be conducted to benefit some at the expense of others (see, for example, Apple 1986; Bowles & Gintis, 1976; Friere, 1985; Giroux, 1981; Willis, 1977), and acceptance of responsibility for the educational structures found in one's own teaching world (Tom, 1984). The quality of deliberation about values and goals also rests on the ability to recognize and conceive alternative valued ends, to weigh each in relation to its own worth as well as its likely consequences for all involved, and to choose among competing goals using higher order moral principles such as justice and fairness. Beginning teachers may be helped to view teaching as a moral activity and assisted in developing appropriate conceptual tools to engage in careful scrutiny of alternative values and goals—most likely those ideas and tools drawn from analytic philosophy, critical hermeneutics, and ethical theory.

Returning to Questions of Means
The more instrumental or technical aspects of teaching assume a different complexion when they are considered in terms of the uncertainties involving both contexts and goals. The theories developed by the new teachers in this study concerning energy appeared to reflect a beginning awareness on their part of the inadequacy of merely employing a problem-solving model in which strategies could be applied systematically to bring about unquestioned goals.

On the other hand, limitations in the kind and depth of the teachers' knowledge and skills (as well as the conditions associated with their novice positions) encouraged them to develop systems for considering and acting on problems that concentrated on particular aspects of context at the expense of others and often resulted in not confronting important moral issues involved in uncertain situations. Theories such as those relating to energy, therefore, appeared to lack the potency that might allow teachers to draw from the different kinds of knowledge and frameworks for thinking that they needed to address fully the uncertain problems they faced. Better systems were called for that opened the possibility of not only using strategies of teaching but that considered these strategies simultaneously in relation to critical contextual factors and important valued ends.

Tom (1984) portrayed such a holistic perspective in his conception of teaching as a moral craft (the craft component encompassing means and contextual elements; the moral concerning values and goals). Van Manen (1977) argued for schema of levels of reflectivity that moved toward greater integration and inclusiveness in ways of knowing. Zeichner and Liston (1987) described a preservice elementary school teacher education program that is designed to promote greater reflectivity and teacher autonomy, as well as appreciation for and participation in democratically oriented educational systems. They cited evidence that the program "encourages students to view their student-teaching context as problematic, to see teachers as moral craftspersons, and to clarify their own chosen perspectives concerning the teacher's role" (p. 40). In another area, secondary curriculum and staff development programs in several states have employed a reflective practical reasoning approach to address the unclear, moral problems encountered by teachers and families (Copa, 1986; Copa et al., in press). Thus, a few conceptual and programmatic models may be found that offer more comprehensive, reflective approaches to the problems of professional practice.

In addition, studies such as that described in this chapter disclose that these holistic models and activities build on, rather than usurp, the natural tendencies and experiences of practitioners faced with unclear moral problems. In doing so, they are likely to offer approaches for viewing and dealing with teaching dilemmas that appear reasonable and potentially useful to teachers themselves. In brief, sound theory making is not separated from—but becomes an integral part of— effective, responsive, moral practice. These are not new ideas, as Popp (1987) observed in his summary of Dewey's primary tenets:

> The following simplifies, but does not oversimplify, Dewey's arguments about education. The reality of life is not the hard objects before us but is found in our choices. When we choose, we must assess our goals, our means, and our context. None of these assessments is easy, but these three elements constitute the fundamental reality of human experience. (p. 149)

Perhaps particularly because these assessments are not easy, they merit further thought and study and hold promise for better ways of thinking about and improving the practice of teaching.

REFERENCES

Apple, M.W. (1986). *Teachers and texts. A political economy of class and gender relations in education.* New York: Routledge and Kegan Paul.

Applegate, J., Flora, R., Johnston, J., Lasley, T., Mager, G., Newman, K., & Ryan, K. (1977). *The first-year teacher study.* Columbus, OH: The Ohio State University. (ERIC Document, ED 135 766).

Arendt, H. (1958). *The human condition.* Chicago: University of Chicago Press.

Barr, A.S., & Rudisill, M. (1930). Inexperienced teachers who fail—and why. *The Nation's Schools, 5,* 30–34.

Berlak, A., & Berlak, H. (1981). *Dilemmas of schooling. Teaching and social change.* London: Methuen.

Beyer, L., & Zeichner, K. (1982). Teacher education and educational foundations: A plea for discontent. *Journal of Teacher Education, 33*(3), 18–23.

Birdwhistell, R. (1970). *Kinesics and context: Essays on body communication.* Philadelphia: University of Pennsylvania Press.

Bolan, R.S. (1980). The practitioner as theorist: The phenomenology of the professional episode. *Journal of the American Planning Association, 46*(3), 259–274.

Bourdieu, P. (1971). Systems of education and systems of thought. In M.F.D. Young (Ed.), *Knowledge and control* (pp. 189–207). London: Collier-Macmillan.

Bowles, S., & Gintis, H. (1976). *Schooling in capitalist America.* New York: Basic Books.

Buchmann, M., & Schwille, J. (1983). Education: The overcoming of experience. *American Journal of Education, 91,* 30–51.

Clark, C.M., & Peterson, P.L. (1986). Teachers' thought process. In M. Wittrock (Ed.), *Handbook of research on teaching* (3rd ed., pp. 255–296). New York: Macmillan.

Comte, A. (1975). *Auguste Comte and Positivism: the essential writings.* G. Lenzer (Ed.). Chicago: University of Chicago Press.

Copa, P.M. (1986). *A route to critical praxis through practical reasoning.* Paper presented to the Eighth Annual Conference on Curriculum Theory and Classroom Practice, Dayton, OH.

Copa, P.M., Hultgren, F.H., & Wilkosz, J. (in press). Transforming thought and action through state curriculum efforts. Critical thinking as a lived activity. In A. Costa (Ed.), *Developing minds. A resource book for teaching thinking* (2nd Ed.). Alexandria, VA: Association for Supervision and Curriculum Development.

Copa, P.M., & Swanson, G.I. (1984). *Making theory in the first year of teaching.* (Report No. NIE-B-81-0108). Washington, DC: National Institute of Education.

Corcoran, E. (1981). Transition shock: The beginning teacher's paradox. *Journal of Teacher Education, 32*(3), 19–23.

Descartes, R. (1969). *The essential Descartes.* New Jersey: New American Library.

Dobbert, M.L. (1982). *Ethnographic research. Theory and application for modern schools and societies.* New York: Praeger Publishers.

Duffy, G.G. (1977). *A study of teacher conceptions of reading.* Paper presented at the National Reading Conference, New Orleans.

Durkheim, E. (1982). *The rules of sociological method and selected texts on sociology and its method.* Steven Lukes (Ed.). New York: The Free Press.

Eisner, E.W. (1984). Can educational research inform educational practice? *Phi Delta Kappan, 65*(7), 447–452.

Elbaz, F. (1983). *Teacher thinking: A study of practical knowledge.* New York: Nichols Publishing Co.

Floden, R.E., & Clark, C.M. (1987). *Preparing teachers for uncertainty.* Paper presented to the World Assembly of the International Council on Education for Teaching. Eindhoven, The Netherlands.

Freire, P. (1985). *The politics of education. Culture, power and liberation.* South Hadley, MA: Bergin & Garvey Publishers, Inc.

Fuller, F.F. (1969). Concerns of teachers: A developmental conceptualization. *American Educational Research Journal, 6,* 207–226.

Gauthier, D.P. (1963). *Practical reasoning. The structure and foundations of prudential and moral arguments and their exemplification in discourse.* Oxford: Oxford University Press.

Giroux, H.A. (1981). *Ideology, culture and the process of schooling.* Philadelphia: Temple University Press.

Glassberg, S. (1980). *A view of the beginning teacher from a developmental perspective.* Paper presented at the American Education Research Association Conference, Boston.

Hoy, W.K. (1968). The influence of experience on the beginning teacher. *School Review, 76,* 312–323.

Hoy, W.K. (1969). Pupil control ideology and organizational socialization: A further examination of the influence of experience on the beginning teacher. *School Review*, 77, 257–265.

Hoy, W., & Rees, R. (1977). The bureaucratic socialization of student teachers. *Journal of Teacher Education*, 28(1), 23–26.

Huberman, M. (1983). Recipes for busy kitchens: A situational analysis of routine knowledge use in schools. *Knowledge: Creation, Diffusion, Utilization, 4*, 478–510.

Iannacone, L. (1963). Student teaching: A transitional stage in the making of a teacher. *Theory into Practice, 2*(2), 52–62.

Jackson, P.W. (1968). *Life in classrooms*. New York: Holt, Rinehart and Winston.

Jackson, P.W. (1986). *The practice of teaching*. Columbia, NY: Teachers College Press.

Janesick, V. (1977). *An ethnographic study of a teacher's classroom perspective*. Doctoral dissertation, Michigan State University.

Johnson, P.O., & Umstattd, J.G. (1932). Classroom difficulties of beginning teachers. *School Review, 40*, 682–686.

Johnston, J.M. (1986–1987). Selected annotated bibliography. *Action in Teacher Education, 8*(4), 81–84.

Johnston, J.M., & Ryan, K. (1983). Research on the beginning teacher; implications for teacher education. In K.R. Howey & W.E. Gardner (Eds.), *The education of teachers. A look ahead* (pp. 136–162). New York: Longman.

Kyte, G.C. (1936). Problems which confront rural school teachers. *Educational Method, 15*, 227.

Lampert, M. (1984). Teaching about thinking and thinking about teaching. *Journal of Curriculum Studies, 16*(1), 1–18.

Lampert, M. (1985). How do teachers manage to teach? Perspectives on problems in practice. *Harvard Educational Review, 55*(2), 178–194.

Lortie, D. (1975). *Schoolteacher*. Chicago: University of Chicago Press.

Maslow, A.H. (1970). *Motivation and personality*. New York: Harper & Row.

Maslow, A.H. (1971). *The further reaches of human nature*. New York: Viking Press.

Mill, J.S. (1959). *A system of logic, ratiocinative and inductive; being a connected view of the principles of evidence and methods of scientific investigation*. New York: Longman Press.

Munby, H. (1982). The place of teachers' beliefs in research on teacher thinking and decision making, and an alternative methodology. *Instructional Science, 11*, 201–225.

Popp, J.A. (1987). If you see John Dewey, tell him we did it. *Educational Theory, 37*(2), 145–152.

Reid, W.A. (1979). Practical reasoning and curriculum theory. In search of a new paradigm. *Curriculum Inquiry, 9*(3), 187–207.

Sarason, S.B. (1982). *The culture of the school and the problem of change* (2nd ed.). Boston: Allyn & Bacon.

Schön, D.A. (1987). *Educating the reflective practitioner*. San Francisco: Jossey-Bass Publishers.

Schön, D.A. (1983). *The reflective practitioner*. New York: Basic Books, Inc.

Schwab, J.J. (1969). The practical: a language for curriculum. *School Review, 78*, 1–23.

Shavelson, R.J., & Stern, P. (1981). Research on teachers' pedagogical thoughts, judgments, decisions, and behavior. *Review of Educational Research, 51*, 455–498.

Sockett, H.T. (1987). Has Shulman got the strategy right? *Harvard Educational Review, 57*(2), 208–219.

Sorenson, G. (1967). What is learned in practice teaching? *Journal of Teacher Education, 18*(2), 173–178.

Spradley, J.P. (1980). *Participant observation*. Chicago: Holt, Rinehart and Winston.

Strickland, E.C. (1956). Orientation programs for new teachers in Ohio Schools. *Educational Research Bulletin, 35,* 169.

Tabachnick, B.R. (1980). Intern teacher roles: Illusion, disillusion and reality. *Journal of Education, 162*(1), 122–137.

Tom, A. (1984). *Teaching as a moral craft.* New York: Longman.

Tower, M.M. (1956). Study of problems of beginning teachers in the Indianapolis public schools. *Educational Administration and Supervision, 42,* 261–273.

Van Manen, M. (1977). Linking ways of knowing with ways of being practical. *Curriculum Inquiry, 6,* 205–228.

Veenman, S. (1984). Perceived problems of beginning teachers. *Review of Educational Research, 54*(2), 143–178.

Wallace, M.S. (1951). Problems experienced by 136 new teachers during their induction into service. *North Central Association Quarterly, 25,* 291–309.

Wey, H.H. (1951). Difficulties of beginning teachers. *School Review, 59,* 32–37.

Willis, P.E. (1977). *Learning to labor.* Farnborough, England: Saxon House.

Zeichner, K.M. (1983). Individual and institutional factors related to the socialization of beginning teachers. In G.A. Griffin & H. Hukill (Eds.), *First Years of teaching: What are the pertinent issues?* Proceedings of a Working Conference, Austin, Texas: The University of Texas at Austin. (ERIC Document, ED 240 109).

Zeichner, K.M., & Liston, D.P. (1987). Teaching student teachers to reflect. *Harvard Educational Review, 57*(1), 23–48.

Chapter 7

Issues in Teaching Practice Supervision Research: A Review of the Literature*

Deanne Boydell

Westminster College, Oxford

The earliest record of student teaching as part of a college-based education dates from the 15th century (Morris, 1974). Today, student teaching is still a major, highly valued component of teacher education (Williams, 1963), but as Wade (1976) pointed out, no other aspect "is so traditionally accepted yet suffers so much from the lack of a theoretical basis with which to support future developments or indeed to justify present ones." (p. 59).

The assumption underlying much current practice is that teaching is best learned by observing practitioners, by serving an apprenticeship with a good teacher. The student teacher "is expected to acquire teaching expertise by watching someone else teach and attempting to go away and do likewise" (Stones, 1984, p. 21). Such an approach implies an essentially passive role for the supervisor as someone who must not interfere "with the guidance of the master and his apprentice" (Stones, 1984, p. 21).

The type of supervision associated historically with the apprenticeship model is still very much in favor, despite the ambiguity inherent in the term *teaching practice* and the existence of ideas that deviate from the model-the-master-teacher approach (Stones & Morris, 1972). In a national survey of teacher education in England and Wales, Yates

---

* An earlier version of this article appeared in *Teaching & Teacher Education, 2*, (2), 115–125. Copyright 1986 by Pergamon Press PLC. Reprinted by permission.

(1982) found that all institutions appointed supervisors; in fact, nearly two thirds used two supervisors per student; for example, a subject tutor and an education tutor. On average, a student supervised by two tutors received one visit per five working days, and a student supervised by one tutor was visited once every 7 days. The average length of teaching practice was 86 working days over a three-year course. The average time allocated to supervision was one hour and 38 minutes for each supervisory school visit. Nationwide, these data clearly represent an enormous investment of time, energy, money, and faith in the importance of the supervision and, for many, the value of the apprenticeship model. How well-founded is this faith?

Despite the growing research interest in many aspects of teacher education (Wragg, 1982), teaching practice supervision has, until relatively recently, received scant attention. Mounting evidence concerning the relative influence of teachers and supervisors on students, however, raises serious implications for the traditional types of teaching practice supervision.

THE RELATIVE INFLUENCE OF TEACHER
AND SUPERVISOR ON THE STUDENT

Research on naturally occurring groups has suggested that both adults and children tend to prefer the psychological intimacy of pairs (James, 1951). Nevertheless, during teaching practice each participant—student, class teacher, and supervisor—has to operate as a member of at least one group of three. Furthermore, the three triad members may be virtual strangers, who differ in backgrounds, perspectives, and expectations, and these differences can lead to conflict. Stones and Morris (1972) reported a good deal of research evidence of conflicting values between students, class teachers, and supervisors. In addition, Booth-royd (1979) found that a) triad members' perceptions of what actually happens during supervision may differ; b) their opinions on the quality of the student's teaching may differ; and c) even if their aims are very similar, they may believe that they are not.

Under these circumstances, how influential can the supervisor be? Morris (1974), in a much quoted study, compared the performance and adjustment (as measured by questionnaires) of two groups of students on teaching practice, one of which received university supervision and one of which did not. She found no significant differences in performance and adjustment between the two groups, although she did point out that Stapleton (1965) had shown that intense supervision resulted in better performance. Furthermore, Martin, Isherwood, and Rapagna (1978) were able to demonstrate that a supervisor can influence students to change in the planned direction of more indirect teaching behavior by adopting a goal-oriented approach.

Despite a few studies like these that show the supervisor can exert a powerful influence, the bulk of the research findings show that the class teacher has a much stronger influence on the student's learning than the supervisor, "even to the extent of negating what the students have learned from their college courses when it runs contrary to the judgments of cooperating teachers" (Emans, 1983, pp. 14–15). Students certainly claim that teachers are more important. In a questionnaire survey of 500 randomly selected students in England and Wales, almost three quarters reported that their cooperating teachers were of greater help than their supervisors (Yates, 1982).

In another study that evaluated an environmental studies course, students indicated the sources of influence on various aspects of their teaching practice. It was found that school practice supervisory tutors contributed significantly to students' evaluation of their work but not to preparation for the practice and task of teaching (Hoste, 1982).

Results such as these raise the question: Given the huge investment of resources in teaching practice supervision, why does the supervisor seem so impotent? Many reasons can be suggested. First, perhaps the supervisor simply lacks time and is reduced, in effect, to a school visitor. Visiting is quite a different activity from supervision. It involves merely social skills, not the "systematic application of knowledge and skills to the solution of classroom instructional problems" (Morris, 1980, p. 149).

Second, the supervisor may be unable to combine satisfactorily the roles of teacher and assessor. Boothroyd (1979) found that the supervisors she interviewed generally emphasized the support functions of supervision but made no mention of the assessment functions. Other research, however, has shown not only that class and student teachers perceived the supervisor as more concerned with evaluation than support but that many students believed that their supervisors had not seen enough of their work to be able to judge them (Yates, 1982). Furthermore, Partington (1982) reported that anxiety related to assessment appeared to be reduced when teachers in schools acted as supervisors. Regardless of the supervisor's claimed emphasis on his or her support functions, students seem to mistrust the supervisor's assessment, and this mistrust could diminish the effectiveness of the supervisor in the eyes of the student (Shipman, 1966) although not his or her perceived power. As Martin, Isherwood, and Rapagna (1978) pointed out, coupling the two roles of supervision and evaluation "gives the supervisor two types of leverage: influence through expertise and influence through power to reward and punish" (p. 86).

Third, it could be argued that the supervisor is removed from what really concerns the student about teaching practice. Morrow and Lane (1983) investigated how students, teachers, and supervisors perceived the instructional problems experienced by the students in teaching practice. Although there was a high level of agreement between students and teachers, supervisors tended to have different views. Apart from lack of time, conflict between the assessment and supportive roles of supervisors, and their remoteness from students' concerns, there is another problem. The supervisor seems unwilling or unable, for a variety of reasons, to help the student make theory-practice connections, to bring the influence of college work into the student's classroom. After studying the expectations of student teaching held by all the participants (supervisors, students, teachers), Griffin (1983) commented: "Attention to the particulars of either research-derived or craft knowledge was conspicuous by its absence" (p. 18). For a variety of reasons (Simon, 1981), there is a dearth of attention to pedagogy (Stones, 1984).

Clearly, all is not well with the traditional styles of teaching practice supervision. When Sorenson (1967) investigated what students think they are expected to learn in teaching practice, he found that students mentioned the application of theory only when warning against it. Following a study of tape-recorded supervisor-teacher conferences, Blumberg (1977) asked "whether or not what currently transpires in many, perhaps most, cases in the name of supervision is not largely ritualistic, deals with a great deal of trivia, and may be considered, at best, non-harmful" (p. 24). To probe further and assess the validity of Blumberg's claim, two approaches are necessary. First, it is essential to examine the dynamics of interpersonal relationships within the supervisor-student-teacher triad. Cope (1969, 1970a, 1970b) suggested the complexity of factors that might be involved. Yee (1968) argued that groups of three are inherently unstable. There is a strong tendency for two members to form a coalition and isolate the third. To what extent does this happen in teaching practice? Second, teaching practice does not take place in a vacuum; it operates in the social setting of a classroom and school. Tinning (1983) asserted that teaching comes under the control of powerful natural forces present in the classroom, and there is a wealth of evidence relating to the socialization of student teachers in schools. Summarizing the results of research in this area, Glassberg and Sprinthall (1980) noted that there was "a multiplicity of concrete and clearly negative findings—student teachers became more authoritarian, rigid, impersonal, restrictive, arbitrary, bureaucratic, and custodial by the end of their student teaching experience" (p. 31). To what extent do sociological factors influence the nature of teaching practice supervision? To what extent can the supervisor counter them?

INTERPERSONAL RELATIONSHIPS: THE SUPERVISOR-STUDENT-TEACHER TRIAD

Zimpher, de Voss, and Nott (1980) argued that despite abundant descriptive data about student teaching, there is a "lack of intimate knowledge about what happens to student teachers, university supervisors, and cooperating teachers" (p. 12). They conducted an intensive exploratory study of one supervisor at work with three students and their class teachers, using observation, tape recording of post-lesson conferences, taped interviews, and written documentation. They found that the supervisor's chief activity was to define and communicate the purposes and expectations to be fulfilled by the student and cooperating teacher. Where the supervisor set low or few expectations, they were exactly met by the student. Following a detailed analysis of the supervisor's role, Zimpher and her colleagues concluded that the student teachers did not understand the criticisms noted by the supervisor, were not able to make any changes in their teaching styles, and were not willing to do anything but satisfy the teacher.

In a recent ethnomethodological study in which six supervisor-student-teacher triads were observed and interviewed during a 4-week teaching practice, the influence of the class teacher was once again apparent: Supervisors were unwilling to say or do anything that would prejudice their relationship with the class teacher. It appeared that the high degree of satisfaction with the quality of personal relationships within each triad might have been achieved at the expense of the intellectual level of discussion between the participants. No thorough discussions of aims or objectives were noted, and no detailed analyses were made of observed lessons (Terrell, Tregaskis, & Boydell, 1985). Follow-up work revealed that supervisors were severely constrained by the lack of a clear framework for the development of students' pedagogic skills (Mansfield, 1986). These findings are in line with those of Griffin (1983), who suggested that if expectations for teaching practice are unclear and imprecise, then the void may be filled by frequent, intense demonstrations of personal regard by the participants.

These results also find support from two studies of supervision that involved taped post-lesson conferences. In one study, teachers were in almost complete agreement as to which types of supervisory behavior they most liked and disliked but made no complaints about the low level of the supervisors' intellectual activity (Perlberg & Theodor, 1975). In the second study, 50 separate supervisor-teacher conferences were analyzed (Blumberg & Cusick, 1970). Although the supervisors and teachers shared the air time equally, only .04% of the supervisors' talking time related to how teachers would go about solving a classroom problem, and only .06% of the teachers' talking time involved asking questions (Blumberg, 1977). The conferences were characterized by such things as distancing, avoidance, ritualism, and "going through the motions" (Blumberg, 1976).

Taken as a whole, the available evidence suggests that the supervisor is isolated intellectually and that distancing devices, such as the avoidance of potentially controversial and threatening debate are needed to sustain the complex working relationships within the triad. In other words, there is no guarantee that a supervisor with unlimited time, great sensitivity to students' concerns, and immense pedagogical expertise would be able to raise the intellectual level of supervision appreciably, given the need for traditional types of assessment and the apprenticeship approach to teaching practice with its brief and transient relationships among triad members.

THE SOCIAL CONTEXT

Morris (1980) made the important point that although some characteristics of supervisory effectiveness are common to various situations, supervisory effectiveness is situational. Copeland (1979) made a similar point about the influence of the social setting on the ability of students to use the skills acquired during training. He argued that this ability depended "not only on the quality of the initial training they receive but on the environment in which they must practice use of those skills, their student teaching classrooms" (p.194).

What are the processes mediating the relationship between the co-operating teacher and the students' use of skills? Clearly a modeling effect may be at work, but both teacher and student may be influenced also by shaping forces within the ecological system of the classroom. In a study of the ability of students to transfer the skill of asking probing questions into the classroom, following microteaching, it was found that the ecological system of the classroom was more important for success than the effect of the teacher (Copeland, 1978). This finding suggests that it may be necessary to look beyond the influence of the class teacher if the social forces at work during student teaching are to be understood, an argument developed by Zeichner (1986).

Friebus (1977) pointed out that although many educational studies of student teaching have looked to the cooperating teacher as the primary socialization agent, student teachers interact with other people, too. Consequently, he interviewed student teachers to find out which individuals were involved in their socialization and the areas in which they made their contributions. The interviews showed that many people, apart from the teacher, were involved in "coaching" and "legitimation," and pupils were almost exclusive referents for the students' images of success or failure, as well as being involved in other contexts. The influence of other student teachers was small. The supervisors' main area of influence was in coaching, but even so, they took second place to the class teacher.

Work on the agents of socialization involved in student teaching relates to wider issues of teacher socialization, such as the widely reported progressive-traditional shift in professional perspectives once either full-time or student teaching starts. For example, when Gibson (1976) followed a group of student teachers through their 3-year course, he found a rapid move away from the notion of teaching as "service" toward a view of school practice as a time for "safety and survival" (p. 24).

Many attempts have been made to explain findings of this kind: Zeichner and Tabachnick (1981) reviewed three different interpretations. The first view is that the liberalization in attitudes acquired during higher education is reversed or washed out by one or more of the agents the teacher comes into contact with in the school. The second view is that liberalism is simply superimposed on traditional perspectives acquired through the largely unconscious internalization of teaching models. In other words, the liberal ideas do not fade because they are never really accepted in the first place, but are jettisoned as they are no longer needed for the purpose of impression management. The third view is that educational institutions do have an impact but not a liberalizing one. The student does not experience in practice the liberalism he or she is freely allowed to express, so the effects of the educational institution actually are strengthened by school experiences. If this latter view is correct, there is a clear implication for the colleges. If the school culture is to be countered, if the college—and the supervisor—are to become more influential, then the colleges need to reform their own teaching (Zeichner & Tabachnick, 1981). One recent study showed that tutors used a limited range of instructional techniques and that their goals were not related to their views about the desirable attributes of successful teachers (Raths & Katz, 1982).

ALTERNATIVE APPROACHES TO SUPERVISION

Given the current state of knowledge about student teaching and the influence of the supervisor, how can colleges and other institutions involved in teacher education respond? Two key points need to be kept in mind. First, teacher preparation is not an ideologically neutral process; it is guided, even if subconsciously, by political and ideological commitments. It should not be assumed that the current systems of teacher preparation or schooling are natural, inevitable, or best. The underlying issues should be debated, and any proposed changes to teaching practice supervision must be seen in this context. In effect, school experience cannot be seen in isolation from theoretical analyses of education as a whole (Beyer & Zeichner, 1982).

Second, it is philosophically unsound to prescribe any course of action as the logical consequence of a given set of facts. The fact that the supervisor appears to have relatively little influence does not logically entail any particular course of action. This section reviews three types of solutions proposed for the problems associated with traditional types of teaching practice supervising: a) abolish the supervisor, b) reconceptualise the supervisor's role vis-à-vis the student, and c) base the supervisor's work in the schools with teachers.

One response to the empirical evidence casting doubt on the value of the supervisor has been the call to enhance the role of the cooperating teachers in the schools (Bowman, 1979). Diamonti (1977) asked: "Is there any evidence to suggest that the student teacher supervisor adds anything of significance beyond what a good master cooperating teacher could offer to a student teacher?" (p. 485). He argued that "it is not appropriate for an institution of higher learning to give academic credit for operating what is basically a placement service that sends students out to sink or swim" (p. 485).

The abolition of supervision would not solve the fundamental problems associated with teaching practice. It would simply shift the thorny questions of assessment to the school and class teacher and enhance the importance of the apprenticeship model. The apprenticeship model is grossly inadequate in several respects (Stones, 1984). First, it leaves students to induce the major attributes of good teaching from what they see the teachers doing, with very little help, a very haphazard and unsatisfactory arrangement because they may see only poor teaching. Second, even if the students observe highly experienced and skilled teachers, they will see only a limited repertoire of techniques reflecting the teachers' own values, experiences, and personalities. These may differ greatly from those of the students and encourage them to copy bits of behavior that are ineffective or harmful in their hands. Third, even if the observed teachers are excellent, it is virtually impossible for any one of them to be excellent on every count. Thus, the students may never be exposed to some aspects of teaching excellence. The fourth and most fundamental flaw of the apprenticeship model is that, despite the burgeoning interest in teaching effectiveness research, there is little agreement as to what constitutes good teaching.

A second suggestion to remedy the deficiencies of teaching practice supervision identified by research has been to reconceptualize the role of the supervisor, and to think critically about the aims and objectives of supervision. Some of the numerous approaches overlap, and each has its own particular emphasis and rationale.

The proposed starting point of one approach is the perspectives and concerns of student teachers. Research has shown that initially students on teaching practice are concerned with "safety and survival" (Gibson, 1976, p. 246). Only later do they turn outward from concerns with their own adequacy to other aspects of teaching practice. In a study of the concerns of postgraduate Certificate in Education students, Taylor (1975) found that as their course progressed, "the once-peripheral concerns with the theory of teaching, with pupils and curriculum take their place alongside concerns with practical teaching capabilities and class control. It is as if the level of early concerns is as much as the graduate can bear in the first part of his training and much of this is taken up in developing a coping strategy" (pp. 157–158).

These findings are in line with those of American studies. Fuller and Bown (1975) hypothesised that there are three levels of concerns development. Student teachers are primarily at the first level of survival or self-oriented concerns. Later, teaching situation concerns appear, and later still comes the third level of pupil concerns. Katz (1972) argued that although mature teacher concerns can emerge by the time teachers have had three years of experience, it may take five years or more for such concerns to appear.

Results of this kind have been taken by some to mean that only survival training should be offered during preservice education (Fuller, Parsons, and Watkins, 1973). Although it is reasonable to suggest that the supervisor is effective "only when he knows and responds to needs of field-based consumers" (Morris, 1980, p. 149), it is debatable whether matching the content of teacher education curricula to the levels of student concerns is the only appropriate response. In the first place, this approach rests on the unproved assumption that current concerns must be resolved before more mature ones can emerge. Even if this assumption were correct, the fact that teachers develop in a certain way does not mean that they ought to be helped to develop in such a manner even if they rate this type of education as highly relevant and feel comfortable with the way their concerns are met. Second, this approach, by seeking to integrate the student into the logic of the existing order, delays the critical consideration of controversial educational issues and may seriously limit the student's professional and intellectual growth (Zeichner & Teitelbaum, 1982).

Although it may be "that students in many colleges and departments of education speak disparagingly of their education courses. . . ." (Taylor, 1975, p. 151), and that teacher educators "teach against the tide," answering very well the questions that students are not asking (Fuller, 1971, quoted by Zeichner & Teitelbaum, 1982, p. 95), the personal concerns approach is seriously flawed. It is possible to acknowledge the importance of students' concerns but focus primarily on fostering inquiry about teaching and the educational and social contexts in which it is embedded. This so-called inquiry-oriented approach at the University of Wisconsin, Madison, assumes that the survival-oriented concerns of teachers are at least partly related to the historically dominant apprenticeship model of student teaching (Zeichner & Teitelbaum, 1982). The apprenticeship model is regarded as inadequate. It is assumed that by replacing it with an inquiry-oriented model, involving high-level reflective activity, students' survival-oriented concerns will become less salient. This particular inquiry approach (Zeichner & Liston, 1987) emphasizes links between everyday teaching and the complex issues of school and society by deliberately structured exercises in inquiry using, for example, ethnographic methods, a theme explored more fully by Gitlin and Teitelbaum (1983). Technical proficiency is still highly valued "but only for its ability to bring about desired ends, not as an end in itself" (Zeichner & Teitelbaum, 1982, p. 102). As such, it stands in marked contrast to a model that is primarily concerned with the technical application of educational knowledge to attain given ends, namely, the competency-based teacher education movement that became popular in the United States during the 1970s.

The competency approach is based on the assumption that teaching can be broken down into sets of hierarchically arranged skills that the student has to master to specified levels. One such list contained more than 1,000 skills (Wragg, 1984). The competency model is open to a number of serious objections (Gitlin, 1981; Heath & Nielson, 1974). First, there are questions relating to the validity of the postulated skills hierarchies. Second, even if these questions could be satisfactorily answered, there are many questions relating to evaluation. For instance, what constitutes acceptable standards of competency and who should establish the criteria? Third, and most fundamentally, it is possible to argue that the teacher "works with more than technical skills" (Gitlin, 1981, p. 47). The competency approach, like the personal concerns and apprenticeship models, diverts attention away from (or delays) high-level reflection on teaching incorporating value judgments and moral and ethical criteria. Insofar as teachers are seen as potential agents of change and improvement in educational settings, this is a fatal flaw.

Competency-based teacher education is by no means the only supervisory approach to focus on teaching skills. Some approaches emphasize technical competency but do so in an inquiry-oriented way, for instance, the Teacher Education Project with its research and development methodology (Wragg, 1984). This open-ended view of learning is also found in the pedagogical and counselling model of teaching practice supervision advocated by Stones (1984).

Stones sees the learning of the pupil, the student teacher, and the supervisor as inquiry-oriented and never complete. It is always subject to further development and refinement by a continuous testing of theory against practice (Stones, 1984, p. 41). Stones' main interest lies in pedagogy, the making of theory-practice links drawing on the large body of knowledge concerning learning, but his approach is broad-based. Under Stones' model, as under the Wisconsin inquiry approach, students are encouraged to reflect on the processes of teacher socialization with respect to their own values and assumptions and to make informed sociological and psychosociological analyses of school and classroom life. Stones argued that these two elements "together with the pedagogical elements, take students into schools not just to observe, but also to appraise, question, evaluate and to experiment in teaching" (Stones, 1984, p. 134).

The counselling component of Stones' model is an adapted form of clinical supervision that originated at Harvard in the 1950s (Cogan, 1976; Goldhammer, 1980). Clinical supervision involves a number of stages, following the establishment of the supervisory relationship in which a supervisor and student are jointly involved in all aspects of the teaching from planning the lessons to the supervisory conference and plans for further teaching. The conferences, which occur both before and after a lesson is taught, lie at the heart of the process (Smyth, 1982). The main argument for clinical supervision is "that if you want teachers to change then it is necessary to *work with them,* rather than *on them!*" (Smyth, 1984, p. 32). Its main aim is to help teachers reduce disparities between their intentions and actions and to become, in the long term, self-monitoring professionals. Its underlying assumption is that "instruction can only be improved by direct feedback to a teacher on aspects of his or her teaching that are of concern to that teacher" (Reavis, 1976, quoted by Smyth, 1982, p. 336).

The feedback provided "has nothing to do with evaluation, inspection or quality control" but aims to improve instruction and promote pupil growth and is based on data arising in the classroom (Smyth, 1982, p. 336). Clinical supervision has been adopted and developed in many teacher education courses (e.g., Gallaher, Romano, Sunflower, & Shepherd, 1983), and although comprehensive empirical support is lacking (Grimmett, 1983), there are indications that it has some success in achieving its aims (Sullivan, 1980). Stones (1984) incorporated many of the features of clinical supervision into his counselling approach but argued persuasively for it to be linked with pedagogy ". . . we must go beyond procedures and cycles and develop the psychological underpinnings of the whole supervisory process" (p. 35).

Stones (1984) shares with Blumberg (1977) the view that assessment, as traditionally understood, should not be part of the supervisor's role, and presented a detailed research-based case for his argument. Blumberg derives his view from his interventionist approach to supervision that emphasizes the socioemotional nature of the supervisory relationship. Although Blumberg pointed out that the supervisor should still be "a competent pedagogical technician" (Blumberg, 1977, p. 27) he saw the supervisor as an interpersonal intervenor, rather than as a methodological and curriculum specialist. The quality of the human relationship between supervisor and student is important. Blumberg believed that in addition to improving the quality of instruction, two additional products should be sought from supervision, namely, the personal and professional growth of both student and supervisor. Against this background, "It seems rather hypocritical and dishonest for a supervisor to engage a teacher in collaborative work and interpersonal effort and then to 'fail' that teacher if these efforts don't pan out productively. After all, it could be that the supervisor failed and not the teacher" (Blumberg, 1977, p. 31).

A common theme running through the approaches that attempt to recast the supervisor's role is the importance of technical expertise. The approaches differ most in their models of human learning, which may be either closed and didactic (Fuller's personalized approach and competency-based teacher education) or open-ended and inquiry-based (Wisconsin approach, Stones' pedagogical and counselling approach, clinical supervision, Blumberg's personal intervention). The approaches also differ greatly in the nature of their evaluatory procedures. Associated with the closed models are traditional types of assessment, whereas the open inquiry-oriented models are characterized by a shift toward diagnostic evaluation. These changes in the nature of evaluation have been accompanied by changes in the extent of the supervisor's active involvement in the teaching practice. With the open models the supervisor has exchanged his or her traditional power relationship for one based, to varying degrees, on collaboration. Teaching practice is held to be beneficial for both student and supervisor.

There is, however, one school of thought that argues that reconceptualizations of the supervisor's role vis-à-vis the student do not go far enough. Drawing on sociological evidence demonstrating the influence of settings, it is argued that before teacher education can have much influence on the student, the schools themselves must change. This line of reasoning gives rise to the third type of response to the perceived deficiencies of traditional teaching practice supervision: The supervisor should give top priority to the teachers in the schools rather than the student (Emans, 1983).

If supervisors are seen as the main change agents for schools and teacher education, their role must be redesigned radically. Emans (1983) described it this way: "College supervisors would still be the liaison between the university and the schools, and would still be available if something goes wrong in the student teaching situation; however, their main influence would be on the cooperating teacher and, indirectly, on the school environment" (p. 16). In more practical terms, Emans suggested that the supervisor should have less direct responsibility for immediate supervision of students, working instead in an inservice mode with teachers on curriculum development and the improving of teaching, focusing on the interpretation of theory and research that constitute the knowledge base of education.

Blurring the distinction between initial and inservice education and reconceptualizing the role of the tutor are major features of the IT-INSET approach (Ashton, Henderson, Merritt, & Mortimer, 1983). With this approach, tutors regularly work with small groups of students and teachers in their own classrooms over a period of time in a selected curricular area. The team members analyze practice, theorize and draw on external theory where relevant, evaluate and develop their work, and, once the pattern is established, involve other school staff. The IT-INSET approach is not primarily a direct response to research findings casting doubt on the validity of traditional types of teaching practice supervision or inservice course work. Instead, it is built on a number of trends in teacher education: "Trends towards a professional focus within initial training, towards school-focused in-service training, to-wards cooperative curriculum evaluation and development, and towards a closer relationship between initial and in-service training . . ." (Ashton et al., 1983, p. 23). In fostering this closer relationship between initial and inservice training, the IT-INSET approach does not see the supervisor as the main change agent for the schools nor the main trainer for the student. Indeed, it is argued that because of an academic background he or she may lack the necessary professional skills. Instead, the training institution-school relationships are seen as cooperative and mutually beneficial. It is argued that tutors (and even their students) have a role in inservice education and that teachers have a no less important role in initial training. Teachers should be helped on a cooperative basis in their own school to engage in a continuing cycle of curriculum development, and student teachers should find in school practice starting points and raw material for their course work.

The IT-INSET approach, along with all other attempts to redefine the supervisor's role, raises a fundamental question. Even if it is

desirable to change the supervisor's role, to what extent is it possible
to do so in practice?

CHANGING THE SUPERVISOR'S ROLE

Advocates of change tend to be pessimistic about their chances of
success. Blumberg (1977) stated that he was not optimistic because of
"too many forces working in a different direction. . . ." (p. 31). He
believed that reconceptualizing the supervisory role would probably
have minimal effect unless other parts of the school system were also
reconceptualized. Emans (1983) wrote that there were many obstacles
to change, not least of which are education staff who "often show little
interest in contributing to, or even using, the knowledge base that
comprises professional education. . . . They see their primary concern
to be with rhetorical teaching and seldom with research production or
theory building" (pp. 16–17). Stones (1984) made a similar point. He
felt the biggest problem to be "the fact that teacher trainers and their
institutions do not perceive there to be a problem." (p. 3).

The task of persuading supervisors to reconsider their role is similar
to that of encouraging class teachers to improve their teaching. In the
first place, the underlying issue is the same: How do you stimulate
reflection on the efficacy of current practice and follow with action
based on this reflection? There is a major problem here. Teachers are
rational in intent rather than behavior, and a major finding of research
on teachers' thinking is that teachers do not follow the traditional
method for instructional design. Instead of specifying objectives, working out procedures for pupils reaching them, and evaluating their
success, they focus on classroom activity and the activity flow (Shavelson & Stern, 1981). How, therefore, can theoretical ideas be linked
to practice? In the second place, the links between intentions and
actions are exceedingly complex (Zeichner & Tabachnick, 1982), and
they are formed in a social context that may inhibit change. This applies
to both teachers and supervisors; in the case of teachers there are some
indications as to what some of these impediments to change may be
(Little, 1982; Smyth, 1984).

There are few obvious rewards—and many associated problems and
dangers—for an educator opening up his or her personal style of teaching
or supervision for discussion and examination. As House (1972) pointed
out, it is easier if he or she "gives lip-service to the idea and drags
both feet" (p. 406). Nevertheless, there is growing evidence that adults
can change. Research on adult learning, although still in its infancy,
"suggests that adults learn in situations where they are provided with
an opportunity for continuous guided reflection, based on 'lived ex-

periences' " (Smyth, 1984, p. 27). Adults need direct, concrete experiences and informal learning situations (Wood & Thompson, 1980). Joyce and Showers (1980) reviewed some 200 inservice courses and found that teachers could be taught new skills and assisted in finetuning their classroom competencies. They discovered five consistent components among the effective programs:

1. presentation of theory or description of skill or strategy;
2. modeling or demonstration of skills or models of teaching;
3. practice in simulated and classroom settings;
4. structured and open-ended feedback (provision of information about performance); and
5. coaching for application (hands-on, in-classroom assistance with the transfer of skills and strategies to the classroom) (p. 380).

Summarizing the evidence, the literature on adult learning holds some promise for those who wish to persuade supervisors to reconceptualize their role, although the existence of formidable problems cannot be denied. The links between thinking and teaching are insufficiently understood, and evidence on the impediments to change in the training institutions is lacking. Nevertheless, enough is known of the conditions conducive to adult learning to warrant a proposal that the training of supervisors be widespread. How this should be done should be a matter for each institution to decide. There is an enormous range of instructional models (Joyce, Weil, & Wald, 1972); of these a collaborative inquiry-based approach involving supervisors, students, and teachers, and a shift toward diagnostic evaluation seem most promising. The choice of a particular training approach is related to how supervision of the student teacher is conceptualized, which, in turn, is related to the instructional model employed in the classroom with children. The very act of setting up a supervisor training program, therefore, may impel an institution to address the issue of providing a theoretical base to teacher education in its entirety, namely, the education of supervisors, students, and teachers.

REFERENCES

Ashton, P.M.E., Henderson, E.S., Merritt, J.E., & Mortimer, D.J. (1983). *Teacher education in the classroom: Initial and in-service.* London and Canberra: Croom Helm.

Beyer, L.E., & Zeichner, K.M. (1982). Teacher training and educational foundations: A plea for discontent. *Journal of Teacher Education, 33,* 18–23.

Blumberg, A. (1976). Supervision: What is and what might be. *Theory into Practice, 15,* 284–292.

Blumberg, A. (1977). Supervision as interpersonal intervention. *Journal of Classroom Interaction, 13,* 23–32.

Blumberg, A., & Cusick, P. (1970). Supervisor-teacher interaction: An analysis of verbal behavior. *Education* (USA), *91,* 126–134.

Boothroyd, W. (1979). Teaching practice supervision: A research report. *British Journal of Teacher Education, 5,* 243–250.

Bowman, N. (1979). College supervision of student teachers: A time to reconsider. *Journal of Teacher Education, 30,* 29–30.

Cogan, M.L. (1976). Rationale for clinical supervision. *Journal of Research and Development in Education, 9,* 3–19.

Cope, E. (1969). Students and school practice. *Education for Teaching, 80,* 25–35.

Cope, E. (1970a). Teacher training and school practice. *Educational Research, 12,* 87–98.

Cope, E. (1970b). Discussions with college and school staff on the subject of "school practice." *Education for Teaching, 81,* 30–37.

Copeland, W.D. (1978). Processes mediating the relationship between cooperating-teacher behavior and student-teacher classroom performance. *Journal of Educational Psychology, 70,* 95–100.

Copeland, W.D. (1979). Student teachers and cooperating teachers: An ecological relationship. *Theory into Practice, 18,* 194–199.

Diamonti, M.C. (1977). Student teacher supervision: A reappraisal. *The Educational Forum, 4,* 477–486.

Emans, R. (1983). Implementing the knowledge base: Redesigning the function of co-operating teachers and college supervisors. *Journal of Teacher Education, 34,* 14–18.

Friebus, R.J. (1977). Agents of socialization involved in student teaching. *Journal of Educational Research, 70,* 263–268.

Fuller, F. (1971). *Relevance for teacher education: A teacher concerns model.* Austin: University of Texas R & D Center for Teacher Education.

Fuller, F.F., Parsons, J.S., & Watkins, J.E. (1973). *Concerns of teachers: Research and reconceptualization.* Austin: University of Texas R & D Center for Teacher Education.

Fuller, F.F., & Bown, O.H. (1975). Becoming a teacher. In K. Ray (Ed.), *Teacher Education, 74th NSSE Yearbook,* (chap. II). Chicago: University of Chicago Press.

Gallaher, J.H., Romano, A.W., Sunflower, C., & Shepherd, G. (1983). A three role group clinical supervision system for student teaching. *Journal of Teacher Education, 34,* 48–51.

Gibson, R. (1976). The effect of school practice: The development of student perspectives. *British Journal of Teacher Education, 2,* 241–250.

Gitlin, A. (1981). Horizontal evaluation: An approach to student teacher supervision. *Journal of Teacher Education, 32,* 47–50.

Gitlin, A., & Teitelbaum, K. (1983). Linking theory and practice: The use of ethnographic methodology by prospective teachers. *Journal of Education for Teaching, 9,* 225–234.

Glassberg, S., & Sprinthall, N.A. (1980). Student teaching: A developmental approach. *Journal of Teacher Education, 31,* 31–38.

Goldhammer, R., Anderson, R.H., & Krajewski, R.J. (1980). *Clinical supervision: Special methods for the supervision of teachers.* New York: Rinehart & Winston.

Griffin, G.A. (1983, April). *Expectations for student teaching: What are they and are they being realized?* Paper presented at the meeting of the American Educational Research Association, Montreal, Canada.

Grimmett, P.P. (1983, April). *"Effective" clinical supervision conference interventions: A preliminary investigation of participants' conceptual functioning.* Paper presented at the meeting of the American Educational Research Association, Montreal, Canada.

Heath, R.W., & Nielson, M.A. (1974). The research basis for performance-based teacher education. *Review of Educational Research, 44,* 463–484.

Hoste, R. (1982). Sources of influence on teaching practice in the evaluation of courses in teacher education. *Journal of Education for Teaching, 8,* 252–261.

House, E.R. (1972). The conscience of educational evaluation. *Teachers College Record, 73,* 405–414.

James, J. (1951). A preliminary study of the size determinant in small group interaction. *American Sociological Review, 16,* 474–477.

Joyce, B.R., Weil, M., & Wald, R. (1972). The training of educators: A structure for pluralism. *Teachers College Record, 73,* 371–391.

Joyce, B., & Showers, B. (1980). Improving in-service training: The message of research. *Educational Leadership, 37,* 379–385.

Katz, L.G. (1972). Developmental stages of preschool teachers. *Elementary School Journal, 73,* 50–54.

Little, J.W. (1982). Norms of collegiality and experimentation: Work-place conditions of school success. *American Educational Research Journal, 19,* 325–340.

Mansfield, P.A. (1986). Patchwork pedagogy: A case study of supervisors' emphasis on pedagogy in post-lesson conferences. *Journal of Education for Teaching, 12,* 259–271.

Martin, Y.M., Isherwood, G.B., & Rapagna, S. (1978). Supervisory effectiveness. *Educational Administration Quarterly, 14,* 74–88.

Morris, J.E. (1980). Evaluating the effectiveness of the university supervisor of student teachers: Role of the coordinator of field experiences. *Peabody Journal of Education, 57,* 148–151.

Morris, J.R. (1974). The effects of the university supervisor on the performance and adjustment of student teachers. *Journal of Educational Research, 67,* 358–362.

Morrow, J.E., & Lane, J.M. (1983). Instructional problems of student teachers: Perceptions of student teachers, supervising teachers and college supervisors. *Action in Teacher Education, 5,* 71–78.

Partington, J. (1982). Teachers in school as teaching practice supervisors. *Journal of Education for Teaching, 8,* 262–274.

Perlberg, A., & Theodor, E. (1975). Patterns and styles in the supervision of teachers. *British Journal of Education for Teaching, 1,* 203–211.

Raths, J.D., & Katz, L.G. (1982). The best of intentions for the education of teachers. *Journal of Education for Teaching, 8,* 275–283.

Shavelson, R.J., & Stern, P. (1981). Research on teachers' pedagogical thoughts, judgments, decisions, and behavior. *Review of Educational Research, 51,* 455–498.

Shipman, M.D. (1966). The assessment of teaching practice. *Education for Teaching, 70,* 28–31.

Simon, B. (1981). Why no pedagogy in England? In B. Simon & W. Taylor (Eds.), *Education for the Eighties* (pp. 124–145). London: Batsford.

Smyth, W.J. (1984). Teachers as collaborative learners in clinical supervision: A state-of-the-art review. *Journal of Education for Teaching, 10,* 24–38.

Smyth, J. (1982). A teacher development approach to bridging the practice-research gap. *Journal of Curriculum Studies, 14,* 331–342.

Sorenson, G. (1967). What is learned in practice teaching? *Journal of Teacher Education, 18,* 173–178.

Stapleton, M.L. (1965). *An evaluation of two programs of student teacher supervision by college supervisors.* Unpublished doctoral dissertation, The Pennsylvania State University, University Park.

Stones, E. (1984). *Supervision in teacher education: A counselling and pedagogical approach.* London: Methuen.

Stones, E., & Morris, S. (1972). *Teaching practice: Problems and perspectives.* London: Methuen.

Sullivan, C.G. (1980). *Clinical supervision: A state of the art review.* Alexandria, VA: Association for Supervision and Curriculum Development.

Taylor, P.H. (1975). A study of the concerns of students on a Post-graduate Certificate in Education course. *British Journal of Teacher Education, 1,* 151–161.

Terrell, C., Tregaskis, O., & Boydell, D. (1985). *Teaching practice supervisors in primary schools: An ethnomethodological perspective* (Research Report). Cheltenham, England: College of St. Paul and St. Mary.

Tinning, R.I. (1983). *Supervision of student teaching: A behavioral critique.* Australia: Deakin University, School of Education.

Wade, B. (1976). Initial teacher education and school experience. *Educational Review, 29,* 58–66.

Williams, R.H. (1963). Professional studies in teacher training—An investigation. *Education for Teaching, 61,* 29–33.

Wood, F.H., & Thompson, S.R. (1980). Guidelines for better staff development. *Educational Leadership, 37,* 374–378.

Wragg, E.C. (1982). *A review of research in teacher education.* Slough, England: NFER-Nelson.

Wragg, E.C. (Ed.) (1984). *Classroom teaching skills: The research findings of the Teacher Education Project.* Beckenham, Kent: Croom Helm.

Yates, J.W. (1982). Student teaching: Results of a recent survey. *Educational Research, 24,* 212–215.

Yee, A.H. (1968). Interpersonal relationships in the student-teaching triad. *Journal of Teacher Education, 19,* 95–112.

Zeichner, K.M. (1986). Content and contexts: Neglected elements in studies of student teaching as an occasion for learning to teach. *Journal of Education for Teaching, 12,* 5–24.

Zeichner, K.M., & Liston, D.P. (1987). Teaching student teachers to reflect. *Harvard Educational Review, 57,* 23–48.

Zeichner, K.M., & Tabachnick, B.R. (1981). Are the effects of university teacher education "washed out" by school experience? *Journal of Teacher Education, 32,* 7–11.

Zeichner, K.M., & Teitelbaum, K. (1982). Personalized and inquiry-oriented teacher education: An analysis of two approaches to the development of curriculum for field-based experiences. *Journal of Education for Teaching, 8,* 95–117.

Zimpher, N.L., de Voss, G.G., & Nott, D.L. (1980). A closer look at university student teacher supervision. *Journal of Teacher Education, 31,* 11–15.

Chapter 8

A Framework for Designing Field Experiences: A Jamaican Study

Hyacinth L. Evans

**Faculty of Education
University of the West Indies**

INTRODUCTION: THE PROBLEM

From the early normal schools to today's teacher preparation programs, field experiences have been accepted as an important and necessary part of teacher education. Some teacher educators and policy-makers recommend extensions of periods of experience in fieldwork. This view of the crucial role of field experiences stems in part from an implicit trust in the value of practical experiences. Yet there is little agreement on the specific objectives of these experiences; as a consequence there is much variation in their nature and conduct (Ryan, 1982, Zeichner, 1984).

Field experience in teacher education is a term that denotes all activities that occur in schools and classrooms. (For other meanings of this and related terms see Copeland, 1981; Nolan, 1982; Warner, Houston, & Cooper, 1977.) They are experiences that allow the student teacher to gain firsthand knowledge of children, classrooms, teachers, and teaching. Early field experience is usually distinguished from student teaching. The former is usually of shorter duration, occurs prior to student teaching, and offers possibilities for a variety of classroom-related activities. The latter requires that the student assumes some responsibility for teaching over a period ranging from 8 to 16 weeks (Hersh, Hull, & Leighton, 1982).

Researchers and practitioners have identified several problems and issues related to the nature, conduct, and outcomes of field experiences in teacher education. For example, there is some evidence that student teaching has little impact on student teachers' perspectives (Tabachnick, Popkewitz, & Zeichner, 1980), and that the potential benefits of early field experience can be compromised by factors such as its timing, the nature of supervision, and the role of the cooperating teacher (Evans, 1986a). In reviewing results of some field studies, Feiman-Nemser (1983) concluded that student teaching may not necessarily help one to become a good teacher. Koehler (1985), in her review of research on preservice teacher education, cited some contradictions in prevailing conceptions of teacher education and the lack of coherence that characterizes student teaching. Others have recognized the many problems inherent in learning from practical experiences (Feiman-Nemser & Buchman, 1983). Many teacher educators, recognizing the traditional nature of field experiences, express doubt about its effectiveness and search for ways to improve what they do.

Research on field experiences has failed to yield results that can serve to point to solutions to these problems and issues, partly because of the weaknesses of the research designs (Ryan, 1982, Koehler, 1985, Zeichner, 1984, 1985). In the case of student teaching in particular, conceptual weakness is reflected in an incomplete or undifferentiated view of the experience (Stones & Morris, 1972, Zeichner, 1980, Ryan, 1982). Another weakness is the study of the effects of student teaching without examining the context of the experience. As a result, there have been calls to attend to the multidimensional reality of field experiences and to identify the curriculum of field experiences (Zeichner, 1984). These calls suggest a need to be clear about what is, can, or should be designed for field experiences.

The purpose of this chapter is to suggest a conceptual framework for making decisions about field experiences in teacher education. In so doing, I am guided by Schwab's (1969, 1971) commonplaces of the curriculum and by his recommendations for the process of curricular decision-making.

A FRAMEWORK FOR CURRICULAR DECISION MAKING

Schwab (1969) discussed the inadequacies of basing curricular decisions on a theory or one theoretical position and advocated instead an emphasis on the practical or the demands of practice. Using practice as a basis for decision making means that one attends to the concrete realities of a particular situation for which a curriculum is to be developed and, as well, engages in the "practical arts for making decisions." Schwab (1971) proposed, as a conceptual framework, four commonplaces of a curriculum—the teacher, the student, the subject matter, and the milieu. That is, every teaching situation includes a teacher, teaching someone—(a student) something—(subject matter) in a particular setting or milieu. Schwab suggested that all four had to be represented in any deliberations about a curriculum. In such deliberations, each representative of each of the four elements would consider and communicate to others the characteristics, special constraints, and demands of each commonplace. Schwab also recommended that representatives assume equality in the decision-making/deliberative process, though circumstances may dictate that one of them predominates (Schwab, 1983).

I use Schwab's four commonplaces as a framework for thinking and making decisions about field experiences. I outline what we know about each commonplace based primarily on research but also on experience as a practicing teacher educator. After the information relative to a commonplace is presented, I use a concrete example of the Jamaican teacher education system to illustrate the ways in which knowledge about that commonplace can inform decision-making and the tensions encountered when all commonplaces have to be considered. In this discussion, decisions about field experiences include not only what students engage in during field experiences—for example, teaching, observation, and the like—but other activities as well that serve to optimize learning from these field experiences.

THE COMMONPLACES AND THEIR CONTRIBUTION TO DECISION MAKING

The Student

Personal characteristics and background experiences. Students enter the field with varying characteristics and dispositions, a result of individual biography, developmental level, and personality. Thies-Sprinthall (1980) contended that variation in level of cognitive development influences one's ability to perceive and respond to problems and to function in complex settings. There is also evidence that the ego identity of student teachers is related to their performance during student teaching (Walter & Stivers, 1977). Coping skills may also enable students to benefit from field experiences (McDonald, 1980).

Previous experience in teacher-like roles (e.g., tutoring, camp counsellor) may develop ideas about teaching that help or hinder openness to learning in the field (Doyle, 1977, Book, Byers, & Freeman, 1984).

Finally, we know that students enter a teacher education program at varying ages and with different educational backgrounds. In some countries, such as Jamaica and some of the other Caribbean countries, students may enter a program immediately after secondary school with a secondary school certificate or its equivalent. In others, such as the United States, the student pursues the teacher education program while he or she is enrolled in an undergraduate university program. In the United Kingdom and some countries of the Caribbean, the student may be a university graduate. In still others, such as Grenada, the student is required to have teaching experience.

Precollege experiences. Students have had several years of participant observation as pupils in classrooms. They have seen examples of teaching from a pupil's affect-laden perspective and have developed preferences on "personal and student-oriented bases" (Lortie, 1975, p.61). They tend to regard such teaching as special and commendable because of personal affection for their former teacher. The teaching practices observed would normally have been current 10, 15, or 20 years prior to their admission to college, and may or may not represent good teaching. As pupils, they were accustomed to looking at the classroom from a single perspective—that of student—focusing on one or two aspects of the situation such as the interest of the lesson or whether homework is assigned. Student teachers bring such limited ways of perceiving the classroom to the teacher education program and the field experience.

Student teachers' perspectives and expectations. Student teachers enter the field situation with definite ideas about what is expected of them and what they expect to do and learn. Expectations may concern their performance or comportment. For example, they may expect to defer to and to please the cooperating teacher, or to teach the way he or she teaches, rather than to change what he or she does. Or they may expect to show mastery from the very start. Such perspectives may limit what students try to do and what they see as legitimate to do; consequently, they may affect what students learn. In early field experience, students may expect to pick up patterns of teaching for immediate application (Evans, 1986a). Such an expectation diverts attention away from inquiring into classroom phenomena, even if such is the stated goal of the early field experience.

Students' perspectives on teaching as a task or as an occupation may also shape their dispositions to learn in the field. In one study, about 90% of the student teachers had high or moderate confidence in their ability to teach at the outset (Book et al., 1983). In another, many students felt that love of children was the most important prerequisite to being able to teach (Lasley, 1980). Such views distilled from prior experiences with and observation of teachers may reduce the whole-heartedness with which they engage in field experiences and the potential learning gained.

Before I describe some of the more relevant characteristics of the student population in the Jamaican case and discuss the implications, I briefly describe the teacher education system being considered.

Jamaica has a three-year teacher education program offered by all teachers' colleges in the country. Students enter the teacher education program with the equivalent of a secondary school certificate. The program allocates 13 weeks to early field experience and student teaching distributed as follows: Year 1—one week of early field experience; Year 2—1 week of early field experience followed immediately by three weeks of student teaching; Year 3—eight weeks of student teaching.

CHARACTERISTICS OF STUDENTS IN THE JAMAICAN CASE: APPLICATION TO DECISION MAKING

The majority of the students who enter the program are young graduates of secondary schools, with little or no experience in teaching. A few may have been involved in Youth Service and/or Sunday School teaching. The majority are graduates of Jamaican primary schools, which are typically teacher and book-centered, with classrooms that have little scope for grouping and individual activities, and where the teacher is a central authority figure. Students regard both periods of student teaching as a time to demonstrate their teaching skills, to be evaluated, and to become certified as a teacher. The early field experience is seen by students and college staff as a preparation for student teaching. There are three significant characteristics of these students that can influence the design of the field experiences: Their precollege experience in classrooms, their perspectives on the purposes of student teaching, and their youth and inexperience.

With respect to precollege experiences, Lortie (1975) argued that students need to gain cognitive control over the unconscious influences of previous models. This is essential if students are to be open to new or alternative pedagogical methods that are different from those they have experienced. He advocated special instructional experiences that challenge preconceptions and internalizations, for unchallenged assumptions may restrict students' openness to learning new or alternative approaches to teaching. It is therefore critical that students engage in activities that challenge and question any assumptions or beliefs about teaching that may be derived from these formative experiences. Such activities could include the viewing and critiquing of videotapes of classroom teaching—including portrayals of the authoritarian teacher-centered and book-centered teaching with which they are familiar. They could also discuss a favorite teacher and the reasons why she or he was liked, or examine their beliefs about the role of the teacher and of teaching and learning. Such opportunities to examine and challenge assumptions and beliefs would be preliminary to their learning about the occupational and technical aspects of the profession, the role of the teacher, and the responsibilities that such a role demands. Activities and discussions that help students challenge and question assumptions would ideally take place during the first year after the period of observation as well as during the second year prior to the early field experience.

Young students who are accustomed to viewing classrooms from a pupil's perspective need to learn to see the classroom in conceptual terms (Copeland, 1981). Their capacity to perceive what is significant can be developed through preparatory activities that precede the early field experience. Such activities include the viewing and discussing of videotapes of teaching and of classrooms and the identification of important aspects of them. Some aspects of the Jamaican classroom include individual differences of children and the challenges they pose, the problems of nonreaders in classrooms, the type and arrangement of desks and chairs and their effect on grouping and pupil-pupil interaction, the effects of noise on teaching and learning, and the various means that teachers devise for coping with limited space and resources.

With respect to student teachers' perspectives and definition of the classroom situation, preparation for early field experience could also include a discussion of their real purpose. The supervisor can be sensitive to or try to discover the student's definition of the situation in both early field experience and student teaching and take this into account in discussions and conferences. For example, if a student regards the early field experience solely as a time to pick up ideas for use during student teaching, the supervisor, knowing this, can broaden the student's perspective by explaining the potential for learning about the challenges of the classroom and the characteristics of children that the experience offers. The expectation that early field experience is a preparation for student teaching is abetted by the sudden assumption of teaching responsibilities immediately after the early field experience. Thus, to optimize learning, early field experience could be separated in time from student teaching in order to allow student teachers time to reflect on and understand the experience and to prevent the direction of their attention solely at what is to follow.

A similar observation can be made with respect to student teachers' preoccupation with evaluation. Such preoccupation focuses the students' attention on what is immediately expedient (e.g., what works, what the classroom teacher approves of) and on what Dewey (1904) called "the outward forms of method" rather than on understanding learning and teaching and advancing pupils' learning. This poses a difficult dilemma for teacher educators. For we cannot dispense with evaluation, because teachers' colleges perform a screening function for the profession. This screening function implies a summative type of evaluation and suggests a compromise in the Jamaican case. Evaluation would be confined to the third year of student teaching. During the second year, evaluation would be replaced by guidance, discussion, and advice, and emphasis would be placed on learning from and experimenting with teaching. The two periods of student teaching would therefore have very different purposes. Another solution to the dilemma of simultaneously providing guidance and conducting evaluation is to broaden what is evaluated during the third year and include such criteria as openness to new ideas and inquiring into one's teaching, in addition to the ability to carry out the tasks of teaching. These additional criteria refer to skills and dispositions that have implications for the teacher's learning from teaching in the long term.

The inexperience of these students suggests a need to introduce them gradually to teaching activities and experiences before they are required to teach. These activities would allow them to lose their initial fears and anxieties of carrying out the tasks of teaching and allow them to develop some easy and basic teaching skills. Microteaching offers one mechanism for achieving these goals. Students who have had previous experience in teacher-like roles (e.g., tutoring) could have the opportunity while in college to examine the differences between such activities and classroom teaching.

The Teacher

In contrast to teaching and learning in regular classrooms, learning during field experiences issues from a variety of agents in and out of the classroom. The field in this case encompasses many areas of the school—classroom, the staff lounge, and faculty meetings, for example. The student learns the norms of the workplace, picking up ideas, assumptions, and attitudes from interactions with a variety of persons in this setting. Despite the multiplicity of influences, I limit these agents to the four that evidence suggests exert the most influence. These are the classroom teacher, the college supervisor, the seminar leader, and the school principal.

The classroom teacher. This person is often assigned the responsibility of guiding the student teacher, acting as a model, and discussing and explaining pedagogical practices. Where the teacher is expected to provide some evaluation of the student teacher, he or she exercises much influence at least for the duration of the field experience (Edgar & Warren, 1969). The influence and power of the classroom (cooperating) teacher have been amply demonstrated (e.g., Karmos & Jacko, 1977). The teacher's conception of his or her role and commitments and priorities in teaching will shape the form and content of teaching and interaction with the student teacher and the pedagogical principles and strategies advocated.

The college supervisor. College supervisors are the most important link between field experiences and the college program. They define and communicate to the school "the purposes and expectations to be filled by the student teacher and the co-operating teacher" (Zimpher, deVoss, & Notl, 1980). The extent of their evaluative power will affect their influence at least in the short term. They can prescribe professional and pedagogical skills and influence beliefs (Karmos & Jacko, 1980) or the rules and principles to follow (Friebus, 1977). They bring their own priorities and commitments, which may modify or extend the aims of a program as formulated by the college (Zeichner & Liston, 1985).

The seminar leader. It is fairly common for college personnel to conduct regular seminars in conjunction with student teaching. The primary purpose of the seminar varies. The seminar leader's interpretation of the purpose, as well as her or his commitments and beliefs, can influence the potential learning. In principle, seminars facilitate student teachers' clarification of issues/problems/questions that emerge in the practical setting. By dint of what he or she encourages, recommends, or admonishes, the seminar leader can reflect orientations to the student teacher's role (e.g., Goodman, 1983), which in turn may influence what is subsequently learned in student teaching.

The principal. This individual wields a great deal of influence in the running of the school. Depending on his or her proclivities or commitments, he or she may work for or against the goals of the college, advocate teaching practices that have little or much educational value, and become involved in or be detached from the student teacher's learning and development. The power and autonomy of the principal and the level of his or her involvement in student teaching varies. In a review of the literature, no research on the principal's influence or impact was found. Nevertheless, the experience of practitioners in Jamaica suggests that this influence is not negligible.

CHARACTERISTICS OF TEACHING AGENTS IN THE
JAMAICAN CASE: APPLICATION TO DECISION MAKING

In the Jamaican program, the classroom teacher is not assigned a formal role during field experiences. During early field experience, he or she is observed by the students without being required to explain or answer questions on what he or she does. During student teaching, he or she may be and is frequently absent from the classroom and is not required to interact with the student teacher. Consequently, he or she will not have the evaluative power that cooperating teachers normally have. Yet, during early field experience, his or her teaching serves as a model to the student teachers. Furthermore, there are a few teachers who do choose to remain in their classrooms when a student teacher is present and be involved in whatever transpires with their pupils. Therefore, we need to consider their characteristics in planning field experiences.

The majority of teachers in Jamaica hold a teacher training certificate, though there are still some untrained teachers in some schools. There exist few opportunities for inservice education. Thus, most teachers have not benefited from continuing education either on-site or in formal courses. There is evidence that there is a high turnover rate among younger teachers and more stability among the older group.

These characteristics suggest that there may be a great difference between what the college and supervisor expect of the student teacher and what classroom teachers do or advocate. Two decisions can be made here. First, the early field experience would emphasize the detection and critique of important aspects of teaching and learning rather than modeling the teacher. Some curricular implications of this stance have been outlined in the discussion of the student commonplace. Secondly, teachers, whether they are given a formal role or not, could be made aware of the goals of student teaching and the pedagogical orientations adopted by the college. With respect to early field experience, the college can inform the classroom teacher of the primary purpose of early field experience, as well as of the specific aspects of the teaching/learning situation to which student teachers are required to attend.

As a policy question, the role and influence of classroom teachers pose another dilemma to teacher educators. Their influence is well documented; this influence can be good or bad depending on the teacher. We know that their actions, attitudes, and expectations are often adopted by the student teacher mainly, no doubt, because of their evaluative power, but also because of positive sentiments and student teacher's perception of what is successful (Hersh, Hull, & Leighton, 1982). Yet when there is no cooperating teacher and student teachers rely on infrequent supervisory visits for guidance, they miss and misinterpret much of what transpires in classrooms (Evans, 1986a, 1986b, 1987). Consequently, the learning from the experience can be compromised. We know that some experienced teachers have a wealth of practical knowledge that can be of value to a student teacher and that teachers can convey with concrete examples and in relation to specific circumstances. But there are also many experienced teachers whose practical knowledge conflicts with what is taught in college. For example, in the Jamaican case, it has been observed that many classroom teachers use traditional chalk-and-talk or expository methods of teaching and engage in very punitive disciplinary action, such as corporal punishment. Pupils rarely engage in discussions. They may spend the major portion of a lesson in copying notes from a book or from the chalkboard. These approaches contrast with teaching methods recommended by the colleges, such as grouping and incorporating pupils' experiences and interpretations in class discussions.

Despite the relative absence of continuing teacher education and the paucity of model teachers, the teacher educator ought to recognize the potential and actual influence of classroom teachers during early field experience and student teaching and assign them a formal role. The challenge then would be to shape the nature of that influence. Research suggests that such efforts have yielded some success (Hersh, Hull, & Leighton, 1982). Changing the nature of the influence would require first that the classroom teachers be carefully chosen and that those chosen be made familiar with the teaching methods recommended by the college. It also requires that they be trained in crucial supervisory skills such as discussing, guiding, and interpreting classroom pehnomena.

It is not easy to create these changes in experienced teachers, especially when they are not obliged by their employing institutions to do so. A formal role for the classroom teacher can pose tensions for the college supervisor and problems for another commonplace—the subject. Differences between the classroom teacher and the college supervisor with respect to teaching goals, methods, and relationship with children can undermine the objectives of student teaching and create problems for the student teacher (Stones & Morris, 1972). These differences and tendencies suggest a need for continuing teacher education in addition to the aforementioned orientation training. Clearly, preservice education becomes more effective when it is planned in conjunction with continuing teacher education.

In Jamaica, college supervisors are also regular tutors at the colleges in both foundations and subject courses. The seminar leader is usually a senior college supervisor and will therefore, be discussed with the college supervisors. Student teachers are normally supervised by more than one college tutor, because there are specialist tutors such as those for reading and mathematics. These college tutors all have at least one university degree, professional certification, and teaching experience. However, there are some who have been trained for the secondary level though they are required to supervise primary-level students. The vast majority of such supervisors have not had special training in supervision.

In the case where college supervisors come from different subject departments and do not have supervision as a primary responsibility, it is important that they develop a consensus on what student teaching is for, what basic methods/procedures will be applied, and what is expected of student teachers. This will not only add coherence to the field experience program but avoid conflicts for the student teacher who is supervised by more than one tutor. This consensus may also minimize conflicts between college supervisors' views and the program objectives (the subject commonplace). Because the research suggests that college supervisors exercise a very powerful influence on student teachers, they need the opportunity to reflect on what it means to teach and to become a teacher and the implications this has for their role as supervisor. These assumptions guide what they do and expect as supervisors, and therefore, need to be made explicit. Such reflection and agreement on goals require group discussion and airing of views. Diversity of views among experienced teachers about teaching is a problem and may jeopardize the coherence of the curriculum. It may even suggest the desirability of more than one aim or orientation in student teaching and supervision.

The characteristics of these supervisors also suggest a need for training in the skills and orientations of supervision as well as in primary teaching for those who lack this background.

The model of supervision has implications for the aims of student teaching. Gaining a consensus on a model of supervision will pose difficulties and may be a source of conflict. Supervisors transfer their accustomed model of teaching to supervision and do not easily conceive of alternatives. The adoption of more than one supervisory model to accord with different aims of student teaching is one solution to this diversity.

Principals often have definite ideas about teaching methods, pupil behavior, and comportment in classrooms that can influence what can be attempted during student teaching and that may conflict with the expectations of the college. For example, if a principal believes that children should start sounding out words as soon as they enter grade 1, and the college strongly advocates reading readiness exercises, there will be conflict, and the student teacher's experience will be compromised. Some principals see as their responsibility the scrutiny and correction of student teachers' lesson plans and the offering of advice and suggestions. Because of the variation among principals, it is crucial in planning field experiences to become informed of each principal's orientations, to choose wisely (where choice is possible), and to inform the principals about areas that are crucial to the program. In the Jamaican case, principals are not required to receive student teachers, though many feel morally and professionally obliged to do so. Thus, care, sensitivity, and caution would need to be exercised in informing the principal.

The Milieu
In Schwab's formulation, the milieux in which the child's learning takes place are "manifold, nesting one within another like Chinese boxes", (Schwab, 1973, p.503). In field experiences, these milieux can be restricted to the school setting or extended to the wider culture that inculcates beliefs and values about children, teaching, and learning. Within the school, the setting exists on two levels—the classroom and the wider school setting. In this chapter, I restrict the discussion to the milieu of the classroom setting.

The classroom provides the physical, social, and instructional setting within which teachers teach and pupils learn and interact with one another. It is also potentially the setting where student teachers learn to teach—that is, develop new ideas, conceptions, understandings, and beliefs, as well as skills and attitudes. The characteristics of this milieu determine the kind and range of experiences and hence what is learned. The physical environment of the classroom is a combination of space or size of classroom, the pupil-teacher ratio, the floor space per child (an index of overcrowdedness), light, temperature, color, acoustics, and facilities such as type of furniture and equipment. The instructional or learning environment includes learning materials, textbooks, visual and audiovisual aids, and other objects that can facilitate learning. One or more of these factors can influence the range of instructional options available to the teacher, the possibility of group work, and pupils' responses to instruction. Constraints on instructional possibilities may limit what a student teacher attempts and learns and restrict the range of questions presented. The classroom is "an environment that contains demands . . . and constraints" (Westbury, 1973, p. 100). Demands may be the pupils' abilities or preferences (Copeland, 1980), the teacher's goals and preferences, and the curriculum or the school's philosophy. Constraints may be physical, personal, or instructional. The activity structures that a cooperating teacher adopts can lead to widely different instructional procedures and teaching skills (Doyle, 1977, 1981). Tasks assigned to pupils can, depending on their complexity, engender different thinking processes and responses, thus providing different occasions for studying teaching and pupil learning and leading to different assumptions and beliefs about teaching.

CHARACTERISTICS OF THE MILIEU IN THE JAMAICAN CASE: APPLICATION TO DECISION MAKING

In Jamaica, most classrooms in which field experiences take place are crowded and noisy. They are often separated from adjoining classrooms by a chalkboard and little space. Pupils sit on wooden benches affixed to a desk; this combined desk-bench furniture seats three. This heavy furniture and the limited space make rearrangement and grouping very difficult. The teaching approaches and the methods of discipline have already been described in the section concerning the teacher commonplace. The classroom and instructional characteristics have implications for the content of supervision, the role of the supervisor, and the teacher education curriculum.

Colleges are not in a position to request changes to the classroom or school environment. They depend on the goodwill of schools and have to take the classrooms as they are. Given this milieu, the supervisor's role becomes critical during early field experience. He or she needs to place what transpires in the classroom in a wider and critical perspective, pointing to alternatives and constraints, making interpretations, and indicating the consequences of what is seen. This role is a critical one, because the features of the classroom will appear familiar and normal to student teachers.

With respect to student teaching, the milieu has implications for the range and type of methods that can be implemented, the content of supervision, and the qualities of the supervisor. It means that in the teacher education curriculum, an emphasis will be placed on teaching-learning strategies appropriate for large groups in overcrowded classrooms. Some methods, such as role play, may have to be avoided. Visual aids will become an important aspect of each lesson. The supervisor's experience in such milieux will become crucial. In such situations, know-how and experience with methods, as well as children's behavior, will become a priority.

The milieu poses some demands on and requirements for the college supervisors. Their disposition to be creative, imaginative, and supportive of the student teacher in difficult circumstances will be an important quality. Above all, if the classroom teacher is not assigned a formal role, college supervisors will need to conduct supervision more frequently to make it effective. Tensions may arise from the disparity between the supervisor's professional training and the methods that he or she is obliged to recommend or approve.

The Subject

Schwab's fourth commonplace—the subject matter, or what is taught, comprised two categories—selections from the disciplines or "customary fields of academic enquiry" and "propensities to act or respond to things, persons and events" (Schwab, 1983, p. 249). Thus, Schwab emphasized formal propositional knowledge and dispositions. In the case of field experiences, there is a minimum of disciplinary or propositional knowledge to be considered, though questions related to the teaching of curricular subjects from the disciplines arise. The subject or content of field experiences can be categorized as knowledge, skills, attitudes, and dispositions. The first category includes knowledge of children and their behavior in classrooms, knowledge of the curriculum, knowledge of the effects of teaching methods and teaching ideas, and knowledge of one's own response to or feelings in teaching situations. Skills refer to the discrete acts that form part of teaching and relate to the more general tasks of choosing what to teach, designing a plan for teaching it, and implementing that plan. Dispositions and attitudes exist with respect to children, to the teaching staff, to parents, to the tasks of teaching, and to the profession itself. To some extent, the type and range of the knowledge, skills, attitudes, and dispositions taught or addressed will be determined by the other commonplaces. Discussions of the other commonplaces have demonstrated how decisions taken with respect to those commonplaces can affect the subject commonplace. For example, the milieu can restrict the type of teaching skills attempted and learned.

We have seen that the commonplaces can influence decisions about what is taught and learned in the field. However, the person who designs field experiences needs a focus, a platform (Walker, 1971), or a set of guiding principles. The orientations of student teaching formulated by Zeichner (1985) can be regarded as alternative platforms in teacher education, which can provide a focus for planning field experiences. Each of Zeichner's orientations makes an assumption about what students ought to learn and how they should learn it. The behavioristic orientation emphasizes the "mastery of specific and observable teaching skills and behaviors, . . . the criteria by which success is to be measured are made explicit at the outset." The traditional craft orientation emphasizes the "accumulated wisdom of experienced practitioners," and a master-apprentice relationship is seen as the proper vehicle for transmitting the cultural knowledge possessed by good teachers to the novice. A personalistic orientation emphasizes the development of the student teacher's beliefs, perception, and conception of teaching that will lead to informed and wise judgment. An inquiry-oriented approach emphasizes the development of an enquiring and critical attitude to what one does as a teacher. Each orientation emphasizes different skills, dispositions, and attitudes over, though not at the expense of, others, and indicates the mode of inquiry to be adopted in the supervisory conference.

These four orientations represent choices for the person designing field experiences, each pointing to types of knowledge, skills, attitudes, and dispositions and the extent to which each is emphasized. To choose an orientation, one has to consider the other commonplaces. I use the commonplace milieu to illustrate how one can decide on an orientation for student teaching.

In the Jamaican case, the physical limitations of the classroom and the shortage of learning materials pose limits on the range of teaching strategies that can be employed. Hence, the inquiry-oriented approach may not be fruitful for student teaching. The challenges that this milieu poses suggest that the teacher (whether classroom teacher or college supervisor) has to be flexible in approaches to teaching and be able to draw on practical knowledge of what has been or can be effective in such classrooms. A traditional craft orientation may, therefore, be an appropriate orientation. But this can only be recommended if the college supervisor is the main teaching agent. For, as mentioned earlier, the majority of the classroom teachers use disciplinary and instructional strategies that are at odds with those taught in college. The choice of the traditional craft orientation would also require that there exists a sufficient number of appropriately trained and experienced college supervisors who can visit the student teacher frequently. The size of the class (which may present problems of class control) and the lack of space for grouping may make the behaviorist orientation an appropriate choice. The personalistic orientation recommends itself because it may enable the teacher to cope on a long-term basis in a school system that does not provide much continuing education for teachers. Each orientation has merits and poses problems. The shortage of college supervisors and the infrequency of their visits may preclude the traditional craft. Because the behavioristic orientation appears to be ideologically at odds with the goals recommended for early field experience, this may not be a judicious choice. In the Jamaican case, the personalistic orientation may be the wisest choice—from the point of view of milieu. A similar analysis would be made with respect to the other three commonplaces before a final decision on orientation is made.

This analysis of the Jamaican case has demonstrated that the framework does provide a useful and systematic approach to making decisions about field experiences. It allows the teacher educator to take the specifics of a particular teacher education system into account. Knowledge of each commonplace provides a basis for critiquing existing practice and for suggesting improvements or compromise. By giving equal attention to all the commonplaces, the tensions inherent in their requirements and demands become apparent. The dilemmas involved in designing field experiences become clearer and better understood. The use of the framework could help teacher educators to plan more realistic field experiences, avoiding discrepancies between preparation for the field and the possibilities of the classroom or the supervisors' and students' capabilities. By recognizing in advance the possible tensions created by attention to more than one commonplace, the teacher educator can anticipate problems and think of solutions appropriate for the circumstances.

CONCLUDING COMMENTS

This chapter explored the usefulness of the four commonplaces of the curriculum—the student, the teacher, the milieu, and the subject—as a framework for making decisions about field experiences in teacher education. Knowledge about each commonplace derived from research and from experience was presented. The characteristics of each commonplace in a particular case—that of the teacher education system in Jamaica—were examined. The framework appears useful in analyzing and making decisions about a particular case. The framework can be especially helpful in countries where the teacher education system has special or unique characteristics or where problems of resources and materials exist. It can also provide a basis for critiquing and evaluating present practice or for appraising procedures for making decisions about field experiences.

REFERENCES

Becher, R., & Ade, W. (1982). The relationship of field placement characteristics and students' potential field performance abilities to clinical experience performance ratings. *Journal of Teacher Education, 33*(2), 24–30.

Book, C., Byers, J., & Freeman, D. (1983). Student expectations and teacher education traditions with which we can and cannot live. *Journal of Teacher Education, 34*(1), 9–13.

Copeland, W.D. (1980). Student teachers and co-operating teachers: an ecological analysis. *Theory into Practice, 18*(3), 194–199.

Copeland, W.D. (1981). Clinical experiences in the education of teachers. *Journal of Education for Teaching, 7*(1), 3–16.

Doyle, W. (1977). Learning the classroom environment : An ecological analysis. *Journal of Teacher Education, 28*(6), 51–55.

Doyle, W. (1981). Research on classroom effects. *Journal of Teacher Education, 32*(6), 3–5.

Dewey, J. (1904). The relation of theory to practice in education. *National Society for the Study of Education: Third Yearbook. Part I.* Chicago: University of Chicago Press.

Edgar, D.E., & Warren, R.C. (1969, Fall). Power and autonomy in teacher socialization. *Sociology of Education,* pp. 386–389.

Evans, H. (1986a). How do early field experiences influence the student teacher? *Journal of Education for Teaching, 12*(1), 35–46.

Evans, H. (1986b, October). Peer evaluation: How does it work in student teaching? *Teacher Education,* pp. 61–74.

Evans, H. (1987). A new model of student teaching: Its potential for learning to teach. *Cambridge Journal of Education,* pp. 120–126.

Feiman-Nemser, S. (1983). *Learning to teach.* (Occasional Paper No. 64.) East Lansing MI: Institute for Research on Teaching.

Feiman-Nemser, S., & Buchman, M. (1983). *Pitfalls of experience in teacher preparation.* (Occasional Paper No. 65.) East Lansing MI: Institute for Research on Teaching.

Friebus, R.J. (1977). Agents of socialization involved in student teaching. *Journal of Educational Research, 70*(5), 263–268.

Goffman, E. (1969). *The Presentation of self in everyday life.* London: Allen.

Goodman, J. (1983). The seminar's role in the education of student teachers—a case study. *Journal of Teacher Education, 34*(3), 44–49.

Hersh, R., Hull, R., & Leighton, M. (1982). Student teaching. In H. Mitzel (Ed.), *Encyclopedia of educational research* (5th ed.). New York: The Free Press.

Karmos, A., & Jacko, C. (1977). The role of significant others during the student teaching experience. *Journal of Teacher Education, 28*(5), 51–55.

Koehler, V. (1985). Research on pre-service teacher education. *Journal of Teacher Education, 36*(1), 23–30.

Lasley, T.J. (1980). Pre-service teacher beliefs about teaching. *Journal of Teacher Education, 31*(4), 38–41.

Lortie, D. (1975). *School teacher: A sociological study.* Chicago: University of Chicago Press.

McDonald, F. (1980). The problems of beginning teachers: A crisis in training. *Study of induction programs for beginning teachers, Vol. 1.* Princeton, NJ: ETS. (Cited in K. Zeichner (1984) *op cit.*)

Nolan, J.F. (1982). Professional laboratory experiences: The missing link in teacher education. *Journal of Teacher Education, 33*(4), 49–52.

Olson, D.R., & Bruner, J. (1974). Learning through experience and learning through media. In D.R. Olson (Ed.), *Media and symbols: The forms of expression, communication and education.* (73rd Yearbook of the NSSE.) Chicago: University of Chicago Press.

Ryan, T. (1982). Field experiences in teacher education. In H. Mitzel (Ed.), *Encyclopedia of educational research* (5th ed.). New York: The Free Press.

Schwab, J. (1969). The Practical: A language for curriculum. *School Review, 78*(1), 1–23.

Schwab, J. (1971). The practical: Arts of electic. *School Review, 79*(4), 493–560.

Schwab, J. (1973). The practical 3: Translation into curriculum. *School Review, 81*(4), 501–522.

Schwab, J. (1983). The practical 4: Something for curriculum professors to do. *Curriculum Inquiry, 13*(3), 239–265.

Stones, E., & Morris, S. (1972). *Teaching practice: Problems and perspectives,* London: Methuen.

Tabachnick, B.R., Popkewitz, T., & Zeichner, K. (1980). Teacher education and the professional perspectives of student teachers. *Interchange, 10*(4), 12–29.

Thies-Sprinthall, L. (1980). Supervision: An educative or mis-educative process? *Journal of Teacher Education, 31*(4), 17–20.

Walker, D. (1971). A naturalistic model for curriculum development. *School Review, 80*(1), 51–66.

Walter, S., & Stivers, E. (1977). The relation of student teacher's classroom behaviour and Ericksonian ego identity. *Journal of Teacher Education, 28*(6), 47–50.

Warner, A.R., Houston, W.R., & Cooper, J.M. (1977). Rethinking the clinical concept in teacher education. *Journal of Teacher Education, 28*(1), 15–18.

Westbury, I. (1973). Conventional classrooms, "open" classrooms and the technology of teaching. *Journal of Curriculum Studies, 5*(2), 99–121.

Zeichner, K.M. (1980). Myths and realities: Field-based experiences in pre-service teacher education. *Journal of Teacher Education, 31*(6), 45–56.

Zeichner, K.M. (1984). *The ecology of field experience: Toward an understanding of the role of field experiences in teacher development.* Paper presented at the annual meeting of the Association of Teacher Educators, New Orleans.

Zeichner, K.M. (1985). *Content and contexts: Neglected elements in studies of student teaching as an occasion for learning to teach.* Paper presented at the annual meeting of the AERA, Chicago.

Zeichner, K.M., & Grant, C. (1981). Biography and social structure in the socialization of student teachers. *Journal of Education for Teaching, 1*(3), 298–314.

Zeichner, K.M., & Liston, D. (1985). *Theory and practice in the evolution of an inquiry-oriented student teaching program.* Paper presented at the annual meeting of the AERA, Chicago.

Zimpher, N.L., de Voss, G.C., & Notl, D.L. (1980). A closer look at University student teacher supervision. *Journal of Teacher Education, 31*(4), 11–16.

Author Index

Subject Index